THE
LITTLE
WAY
OF
ADVENT

meditations in the spirit of
St. Thérèse of Lisieux

FR. GARY CASTER

SERVANT
BOOKS

PUBLISHED BY FRANCISCAN MEDIA
Cincinnati, Ohio

Unless otherwise noted, Scripture passages have been taken from *Lectionary for Mass for Use in the Dioceses of the United States of America,* second typical edition © 2001, 1998, 1997, 1986, 1970 Confraternity of Christian Doctrine, Inc., Washington, D.C. Used with permission. All rights reserved. No portion of this text may be reproduced by any means without permission in writing from the copyright owner. Scripture texts marked *NAB* are taken from the *New American Bible, revised edition* © 2010, 1991, 1986, 1970 Confraternity of Christian Doctrine, Washington, D.C., and are used by permission of the copyright owner. All Rights Reserved. No part of the *New American Bible* may be reproduced in any form without permission in writing from the copyright owner. Excerpts from *Story of a Soul*, translated by John Clarke, O.C.D. Copyright (c) 1975, 1976, 1996 by Washington Province of Discalced Carmelites, ICS Publications, 2131 Lincoln Road, N.E., Washington, DC 20002-1199 U.S.A. www.icspublications.org.

Cover and book design by Mark Sullivan
Cover image © photoXpress | Ivonne Wierink

LIBRARY OF CONGRESS CATALOGING-IN-PUBLICATION DATA
Caster, Gary, 1961-
The little way of Advent : meditations in the spirit of St. Thérèse of Lisieux / Gary Caster.
p. cm.
Includes bibliographical references (p.   ) and index.
ISBN 978-1-61636-169-3 (alk. paper)
1. Advent—Meditations. 2. Christmas—Meditations. 3. Church year meditations. 4. Thérèse, de Lisieux, Saint, 1873-1897. 5. Catholic Church. Lectionary for Mass (U.S.). I. Title.
BX2170.A4C36 2012
242'.33—dc23
2012015130

ISBN 978-1-61636-169-3

Published by Servant Books,
an imprint of Franciscan Media
28 W. Liberty St.
Cincinnati, OH 45202
www.FranciscanMedia.org
www.ServantBooks.org

Printed in the United States of America.
Printed on acid-free paper.

12 13 14 15 16 5 4 3 2 1

DEDICATION

For Nancy L. Bearce,
"You're just the best!"
Requiescat in pace

CONTENTS

Many of us have favorite Christmas memories. We can recall a time when the importance of the season was perfectly reflected in its celebration. Once during an Advent mission at a parish in central California, a fifth-grade student asked about my favorite Christmas.

Without hesitation I told the story of what ended up being the last time my immediate family was able to be together. We were gathered at what was then my parents' new house. As there were many fond memories from the home in which we had been raised, I know my mother was concerned about what this Christmas might be like.

As we gathered around the Christmas tree, the five of us grown children found our stockings placed atop trunks. Now, my mother was known for her skill in finding things for our stockings, so we were intrigued as to what the trunks might hold. We were eager to open them, and my parents only excited our child-like enthusiasm by making us open first the presents beneath the tree. The wait was unbearable.

Finally it was time to open the trunks. What we discovered was truly remarkable. My parents had saved items from our childhood, adolescence, and even our young adulthood. There were projects from kindergarten and grade school, school papers, newspaper clippings, and photos—most of them long forgotten. Included in my trunk was the Bible that once belonged to the deceased pastor of our parish; he had been my first spiritual director. Each item sparked a conversation, an exchange of memories. We laughed, shared, and reminisced well into the day.

During the season of Advent, the Church opens Scripture like a trunk stored with articles from her past. We are asked to look back on the signs and wonders God has worked in order to draw the strength and courage we need while awaiting his return. The prophet Isaiah describes salvation in the most reassuring terms, while the daily Gospel passages confirm its fulfillment in the Person of Christ. The way we take time to look back, reflect upon, and share what God has done determines how we will celebrate the strong and powerful God coming to us in the vulnerability of a child.

The Little Way

For St. Thérèse of Lisieux, the most remarkable Christmas experience was in 1886, when she was thirteen years old. That was the day of her "complete conversion," the day she received the "grace of leaving my childhood."[1]

The youngest of nine children, one of five surviving daughters, Thérèse was surrounded throughout her life with love.[2] The care of her elder sisters and the doting affection of her father made her unaccustomed to doing things for herself. The failure of her family to notice the times she was able to accomplish some little act on her own would lead her to tears. She was often told that because she shed so many tears in childhood, there would be none to shed later on.

Prior to what she calls her "Christmas miracle," Thérèse would describe herself as being extremely touchy. More than anything, she despised causing anyone she loved "some little trouble." She wanted to overcome this fault but knew that only God could make her "grow up in an instant."

So it was that Thérèse returned from Christmas Eve Mass excited to see the presents filling her shoes. This had always been an occasion on which her father took great delight. This Christmas, however, Jesus was to show Thérèse that she was to "give up the defects of her childhood." Rather than being excited about watching his daughter discover what "the magic shoes held," her father was annoyed, hoping that this would "be the last year" for such childish pleasures.

Thérèse's heart was pierced at overhearing these words as she went upstairs, and tears began "glistening in her eyes." Her sister Celine encouraged her not to go back down, but Jesus changed Thérèse's heart. She forced back her tears, went downstairs, and placed her shoes in front of her father, there to remove "joyfully" all the objects. "Papa was laughing; Celine believed it was all a *dream!*"

Thus on the night when Jesus "made Himself subject to *weakness* and suffering" for love of us, he made Thérèse strong and courageous, and the source of her tears was dried up. From this day forward she was to walk "from victory to victory."[3]

In a sense the season of Advent encourages us to grow up. We are to set aside whatever may be sources of spiritual touchiness. We look back at what was in order to regain a proper sense of what is, especially as the arduous moments of life can cloud our vision. By immersing our lives in the rhythm of the season, charity can flood our souls and fill us with the happiness for which we were created. We awake Christmas morning prepared to celebrate the birth of our Savior not as a memory but as a profound experience of God's redemptive love, with which the

Scriptures of Advent have saturated us. It is a love that defies all expectations.

This love is what enables us to look ahead to Christ's return. Christians "stand erect" before God; we do not grovel. We know what God is up to in Christ; we know that he is always on our side. We look ahead in hope, because the presence of God in Christ, a presence to which we now have access, determines how we live. Human weakness no longer needs to limit our experience of God's presence in Christ. Our ability to navigate between the past, with its prophetic descriptions, and the future, with its apocalyptic shadings, is wholly dependent upon the fact that God has always been one step ahead of us. His plan transcends even our greatest desires.

Christmas and the Cross

What the saint of the Little Way describes as a miracle is the essence of Christmas. God comes to us in the Person of his Son, to pierce our hearts and fill them with his life. He comes to challenge every idea we have about ourselves and others by challenging our ideas of him.

This is the focal point of the Christmas narrative. A virgin and a righteous man found themselves welcoming new life far away from family and friends. How could it be that the greatest moment of human existence was celebrated with humble shepherds and barnyard animals? Their situation challenged their ideas of God and of themselves. This pattern continued, as together they remained faithful to the God who brought them together.

It had to be this way, because the child they welcomed was born to suffer. The weak, vulnerable child reaching out for love, comfort, and protection was already showing the world how

God's love would be revealed. The child born on Christmas Day is the same man whose lifeless body would hang upon a cross.

This is why Thérèse took as her religious name "Thérèse of the Child Jesus and the Holy Face." She knew that the attractiveness of the child is meant to draw us into the mystery of redemptive suffering. She knew that Christmas and the cross are inseparable moments. Throughout her life she would learn to recognize in the light shining from the child Jesus how to cherish what's essential by embracing what is difficult.

When I was a young priest, I concelebrated a Christmas Mass at which a young girl was asked to bring the child Jesus to the manger. We suffered a delay because the girl refused to do so unless Jesus was on a cross. She recognized what Thérèse had discovered on her favorite Christmas Day—namely, that love is revealed through sacrifice.

Christmas is not the remembrance of something that happened in the past but the celebration of the way of life to which each one of us is called. We bring ourselves before the child to discover the hidden God humbling himself before the human family—naked, weak, hungry, and in need. If we can see the face of God in the child whose birth we celebrate, then we will see the face of God in the man whose death has set us free, whose blood inebriates our hearts and causes them to sing,

> Glory to God in the highest
> and on earth peace to those on whom his favor rests.
> (Luke 2:14, *NAB*)

Sunday, Week One, Cycle A
  First Reading: Isaiah 2:1–5
  Second Reading: Romans 13:11–14
  Gospel: Matthew 24:37–44

Expect Everything

The description of how things will be when the Son of Man returns should come as little surprise. Those who are eating, drinking, and taking spouses suspect nothing; they have already decided that their expectation for unending happiness is an illusion, that nothing can truly fulfill them. They make choices according to physical, emotional, and social desires.

Jesus compares them to the people who lived in the days of Noah. These people could not see past themselves to even glimpse the God who towers high above the mountains. They had completely lost their perspective and thus could not recognize their desire for happiness as a desire for God.

St. Paul accurately described this condition as "sleep." It was the condition of many in the Roman community. St. Paul knew that once we turn our gaze from the Person of Jesus, darkness comes upon us. Promiscuity, licentiousness, wrangling, and jealousies all stem from this fundamental loss of perspective. Instead of seeking a relationship with the only One who can fulfill us, we direct our life toward immediate and ever-changing desires. We trade the glory of being created for God for the futility of making a life for ourselves.

When disappointment ends up determining and limiting life, the light of the Lord can be extinguished. The horizon of human potential recedes from view. We expect nothing greater or more beautiful than that which we can construct—however fleetingly—for ourselves.

The season of Advent is meant to establish our true horizon with greater clarity. For those who have lost perspective, the season proposes a method for reclaiming it. That method involves both a look back to the expectations of the Israelites and a look forward to the return of the Son of Man.

Christians may not know when the Master is coming, but they know that he is coming. This conviction secures our Christian identity. It fixes us within the relationship that perfectly defines what it means to be human and fully alive: a relationship with God.

This relationship that Christ makes possible satisfies the expectations in the human heart. As it does so, the heart expands. The longing for Christ's return grows into a longing for an infinite and ever-deeper relationship with God.

St. Thérèse understood that looking ahead to Christ's return keeps us awake and attentive. She could celebrate God's coming as a man because the gift of Jesus's life opened her to the ways of God and enabled her to walk along his paths—not side by side but through, with, and in him.

It is with joy I shall contemplate You on the Last Day.

Sunday, Week One, Cycle B
   First Reading: Isaiah 63:16b–17, 19b; 64:2–7
   Second Reading: 1 Corinthians 1:3–9
   Gospel: Mark 13:33–37

Standing Before Reality

In today's Gospel Jesus provides the most succinct description of how Christians are to live in the world: "watchful" and "alert." Christianity is not the stuff of dreams and illusory hopes. Christianity entails being grounded in and open to reality.

As St. Paul reminds the Corinthians, every gift of the Spirit has been given precisely so that Christian men and women can stand before the world, without blame, as witnesses to Christ. The enrichment of the Spirit allows each member of Christ's body to remain joined to the Son. It is exactly this communion that facilitates God's presence in the world, a presence that perfectly corresponds with the heart's desire for truth, happiness, goodness, justice, peace, and beauty.

The prophet Isaiah describes how the people of Israel awakened to the reality of their sinful condition. Rather than pushing them away from God, this truth brought them back! They longed to have God "rend the heavens and come down." Awakened to the truth of their sin and its power over them, they recalled the God who was Redeemer and cried out for the security of his presence.

During Advent the Church celebrates God's unimaginable response to the people's cry for salvation. In the Person of his Son, God comes to us as we are. Jesus is the perfect way for us to see the Lord's face and thus be redeemed. Jesus is the human face of

God, and Advent celebrates how wonderfully God has returned to the tribes of his inheritance. This is not a dream; this is reality.

During the season of Advent, the Church also celebrates the enduring presence of God mediated through Christ's body, the Church. We are not awaiting the return of a master who has abandoned us. If that were true it would be preferable to sleep until his return; after all, without him we can do nothing (see John 15:5). Rather we long for all things to be consumed by the presence that has consumed our lives. Knowing that Christ alone redeems and fully restores all the works of God's hands, we await his return so that "God may be all in all" (1 Corinthians 15:28, *NAB*).

Being awake means standing unafraid before reality—unafraid of the limitations, weaknesses, and sins in ourselves, in others, and in the social structures our hands have made. It means being unafraid of the created order's continuing journey. If we are awake as Jesus commands us to be, we will stand positive and filled with hope.

This is the brilliance of the little way of spiritual childhood. It is not a program for moral perfection; it is the fitting disposition of the Christian. It is the way of the one who stays awake.

Ah! The Lord is so good to me that it is quite impossible for me to fear Him.

Sunday, Week One, Cycle C
   First Reading: Jeremiah 33:14–16
   Second Reading: 1 Thessalonians 3:12—4:2
   Gospel: Luke 21:25–28, 34–36

Living in the Present

Today's readings are great examples of the movement that takes place during this first season of the liturgical year. While it can be confusing to look back to the time prior to Christ's birth and forward to the time when he will come in glory, the goal is to focus our attention on the present.

We know that the words of the prophets have not completely come to pass. The lion and the lamb have never slept together, and the viper has never played in the cradle of a child. Judah is not safe, nor is Jerusalem secure. The prophet's careful choice of words was meant to prepare the people for the unimaginable way in which God would restore them. We look back in order to stand with confidence as we look ahead to the coming of the Son of Man.

We can't properly appreciate the presence of God as man. It indeed is more heaven-shaking than the "signs in the sun, the moon, and the stars." To contemplate it is to saturate our minds with a picture of God's redemptive love. It is a love that defies all expectations.

Jesus does not point our attention to the future in order to frighten us into submission. He has us look ahead because what is promised in the future is just as unimaginable as was his first coming. And looking ahead will determine how we live right now. Hopefully it will guard our hearts from becoming coarsened through "carousing and drunkenness and the anxieties of daily life."

We look ahead to the coming of the Son of Man, standing erect and with heads held high. We live in hope, not in fear. Our experience of God is no longer limited by human weakness or even human sinfulness. God has always been one step ahead of us, with a plan that exceeds our greatest desires.

The Little Way helps us move through Advent with our focus on God's presence. The birth of Christ exceeded the expectations of the chosen people, so we do not fear the coming of the Son of Man but rather welcome it. This conviction should overflow into our present moments and resonate with the ecstatic noise of angels singing.

My heart overflows with gratitude when I think of this inestimable treasure which must cause a holy jealousy to the angels of the heavenly court.

December 8: The Solemnity of the Immaculate Conception
  First Reading: Genesis 3:9–15, 20
  Second Reading: Ephesians 1:3–6, 11–12
  Gospel: Luke 1:26–38

God's Yes

To dismiss out of hand God's direct action in the generation of Mary's human life is nothing less than an attempt to push his direct action from all aspects of human life. To say that God could not have created Mary free from the stain of original sin is ultimately a refusal to believe that he can save us. If he can act in history, then his ability to do so is wholly open-ended.

Mary experienced the truth of God's action in history not as a theoretical or conceptual abstraction but as a fact—as real as her own flesh and blood and her fertility. Her yes to God is much more than the mere willingness to follow a preordained program; it is the original existential grounding of human life. Her openness to God perfectly reflects and acknowledges God's openness to humanity. Creation was intentionally and by design open to God; that's why we can say, "God is love" (1 John 4:8, *NAB*). In fact, we can say that creation *is* only because God said yes.

So Mary's yes to God is in no way a renunciation of any aspect of her humanity. Neither is our yes to God. Saying yes to God is the only way to be fully human, the only way to experience exactly what God was up to when he said, "Let there be…," and it happened (see Genesis 1). Mary perfectly expresses this creative yes when she says, "May it be done to me…," and it happens.

The yes Mary speaks to God is the word he has been waiting to hear from the creation he so loves. God's timeless and irrevocable yes meets Mary's yes, and so the wedding of God and humanity literally comes to life. Jesus is the Incarnation of God's creative yes and creation's yes back through Mary. In this union of words, all things are possible—miracles, salvation, redemption, and most especially human love.

Whenever our fragile humanity and sinful inclinations stir up a hint of renunciation, we have only to look at Mary. This woman will always encourage us to stand in the presence of God's generative yes and be transformed. For she gave God's yes a name and face, a biography and history, her flesh and blood.

I prefer to agree very simply that the Almighty has done great things in the soul of His divine Mother's child.

Monday, Week One
First Reading: Isaiah 2:1–5
Alternate Reading in Year A: Isaiah 4:2–6
Gospel: Matthew 8:5–11

Refuge and Cover

Looking back to the first coming of Christ and forward to his return should fix within our minds the depths of God's love. In his encounter with the centurion, Jesus makes it abundantly clear that faith is rooted in absolute dependence on God. Only a person who understands that Jesus came into the world to wash away our filth and cleanse us of the blood shed in our midst would dare to echo the request of the centurion in today's Gospel.

The man comes out to meet Jesus filled with confidence. There is something about Jesus that matches his own experience, and he explains this to the Lord. In the end Jesus praises him and holds him up as a fitting model of a child of Abraham. The centurion's unworthiness is not what moves the Lord's heart; rather it is the man's willingness to entrust his need to Jesus.

It is trust alone that binds our lives with the life of Christ, like branches on the vine (see John 15). All who share life with Christ become the fruit of the earth, for they possess the same beauty and glory as Christ. By radically accepting that the word of Jesus suffices in every circumstance and in all troubling situations, human life becomes open to the glory that belongs to God alone. Thus the feast that has been set for Abraham, Isaac, and Jacob is enormously vast. It is meant for all—"from the east and the west"—who have placed their trust in God. It is for all those who long to live under the canopy of the glory of the Lord.

Through his humanity Jesus was able to reveal the singular destiny of all women and men. He offered himself as both the concrete sign of this destiny and the means of achieving it. By entering under the roof of human history, Jesus came to us exactly where we lay ill and gave his own life as the cure for our fallen condition.

God the Father wasn't content to send a message of healing to the human family. His love was so great that he sent us his Son— "a man like us in all things but sin" (Eucharistic Prayer IV)— as the definitive expression of his unrelenting love. It was our unworthiness that stirred God to respond, not our merits or our goodness. Thus to understand the nature of the feast that has been prepared for us, we need to look back to that moment when the Son pitched his tent among us (see John 1:14). And knowing that Christ will bring to fulfillment on his return all that his birth initiated should bring us "rejoicing to the house of the Lord" (Psalm 122:1).

Awaiting the Lord's return is not a matter of hoping against all odds that we might live eternally with him. Rather it means living now the assurance that God will bring to fruition the true purposes of his Son's coming. We will know and possess God as God knows and possesses himself.

You know, O my God, I have never desired anything but to love You, and I am ambitious for no other glory.

Tuesday, Week One
First Reading: Isaiah 11:1–10
Gospel: Luke 10:21–24

God Notices Us

Listening to Jesus's words in the Gospel, it isn't hard to imagine that the apostles must have asked themselves, "What have we seen?" Although they had witnessed miracles, they knew that Jesus had something greater in mind.

In time, and through the gifts of the Holy Spirit, the apostles would come to appreciate that in accompanying Jesus on his public ministry, they were eyewitnesses of God's fulfillment of Isaiah's words in today's First Reading. In Jesus the apostles encountered the presence of God in a way that turned the world on its head, that went so far as to eliminate even natural predations. What was revealed to the apostles has likewise been revealed to the unlearned and "the childlike": God is not an enemy of man!

God so loves the world that he was willing to become one with us in his Son, to whom all things have been handed over. We need never fear the God who created us, the God whose love we often take for granted and even sometimes ignore. None of this matters to God! All that matters is that we discover the truth of ourselves in him.

What has been revealed to the apostles and the childlike is that God never fails to notice us. This is the foundation for the justice Christ brings. His justice does not destroy or disfigure but rather builds up and makes beautiful. God does not judge me by hearsay but according to the truth in my heart.

The one whom God raised from the stump of Jesse has come to gather, not scatter, to bind up wounds, free captives, and allow the deaf to hear and the lame to leap like stags. If we understand just what God is up to in Christ, then our eyes will see that for which the prophets longed, and our ears will hear what they strained to hear.

In celebrating the birth of Christ, let us carefully consider what his birth reveals about God. This is a God who comes not to condemn but to give life. Once we begin to grasp this life, then the vision of Isaiah, as remarkable as it seems, cannot hold a candle to the light that will shine from us.

Oh! how happy I am to see myself imperfect and to be in need of God's mercy.

Wednesday, Week One
  First Reading: Isaiah 25:6–10a
  Gospel: Matthew 15:29–37

Healing Is Not Enough

In today's Gospel Jesus goes up the mountain and reveals the banquet "of rich food and choice wines" that the Lord of Hosts has prepared for all people. The lame, the crippled, the blind, and the dumb truly have their mourning veil removed and their tears wiped away. Their physical transformation exposes their hearts to the spiritual truth that underlies Jesus's power to heal. In the moment of their deliverance from the limitations and imperfections of their physical bodies, they can cry out, "Behold our God!"

On the mountain by the Sea of Galilee, the great crowd is amazed to see the human face of God in the man who is "moved with pity for the crowd." The loaves and fishes he blesses and shares signify something even greater than the words of the prophet Isaiah. They point to the mountain on which the Father's meal will be served, the mountain of Calvary. That is the place Isaiah had in mind when he foretold how God would take away the shame of his people.

The hand of the Lord rests on the mountain of Calvary; it is from there we are fed. The rich and juicy food is the Body of Christ, and the fine strained wine is his Blood. Those who allow themselves to be fed on this mountain truly rejoice, for the meal of which they eat their fill is the sacrifice that has brought salvation.

Jesus continues to lead crowds to green pastures. He continues to revive empty souls and drooping spirits by the banquet of his

Body and Blood, which his disciples—the Church—continue to set before the hungering multitude. All who sit and eat will be satisfied, and their cups will overflow.

We are all crippled, lame, blind, and mute. Each of us longs for the "restful waters" that well up to everlasting life (Psalm 23:2). Jesus came to heal wounds that penetrate deeper than the flesh. He came to satisfy our hunger for goodness, peace, justice, happiness, beauty, love, and joy. By the sacrifice of his life, Jesus has destroyed death and opened for us "the house of the LORD," where we are to dwell forever.

The hill of Calvary is the "mountain [of] the LORD of hosts." It is the only place to find the Lord for whom we look; it is the only place to exult and praise God. It is the place on which "the hand of the LORD will rest."

Our Lord died on the Cross in anguish, and yet His was the most beautiful death of love.

Thursday, Week One
First Reading: Isaiah 26:1–6
Gospel: Matthew 7:21, 24–27

Letting the Lord Lift Us
Working daily to maintain status and reinforce lofty positions is tiresome; it wearies the soul. Some who try to live high might trample on others. As they struggle to give their lives purpose, they may cry out, "Lord, Lord," but they will not "enter the Kingdom of heaven."

The "strong city" set up by the Father is for the "nation that is just, one that keeps faith." Only those who have discovered in the words of Jesus the firm foundation on which a full and vibrant life is built can stand before God and cry out, "Open up the gates!"

Jesus tells us in the Gospel that the surest sign of trust is the willingness to do the will of his Father in heaven. Thus our lives should be formed and built upon the word that Jesus speaks both in our inner hearts and in the Church that is his body. Only his words can lift us up and set our lives on the path that leads straight through the gates of holiness. Only his words give true meaning and definitive purpose to our lives. Only the words of Jesus can move us away from the spiritual impoverishment that is our fallen condition.

The kingdom of heaven is more than just a place where we hope to live forever. It is the way we want to *be* forever. The kingdom of heaven is a communion of lives that steadfastly yield to the Rock, that take refuge in the Lord and not in men, and that willingly accept all that the Father asks of them. The kingdom of heaven is not merely a hope for an afterlife; it is the way of life for those who know that the love of God endures forever.

In looking back on the first coming of the Son of Man, we discover in his life the truth of our lives. We encounter the height and breadth and depth of God's love through his Son's willingness to do whatever the Father asked him. Jesus's trust in the Father reconciled us with God; it is therefore the only way of living our reconciliation with him.

Jesus lived his earthly life within the kingdom of heaven, and he came as the gateway by which we, too, can enter that kingdom and dwell eternally with God. We look forward to his coming again in glory, ready and eager to sing out, "Blessed is he who comes in the name of the LORD."

Jesus came to lift us up and set us on the loftiest place imaginable, the place where he is seated at God's right hand. Being there with him enables us to do the will of the Father and to trample whatever may oppose him.

I applied myself especially to loving God, and it is in loving him that I understood my love was not to be expressed only in words, for: "It is not those who say: 'Lord, Lord!' who will enter the kingdom of heaven, but those who do the will of my Father in heaven."

Friday, Week One
First Reading: Isaiah 29:17–24
Gospel: Matthew 9:27–31

The End of Tyranny

Once more the words of the prophet Isaiah describe the condition of fallen humanity and God's plan to set things right. The time between our rejection of God and the coming of the Son of Man may have seemed long, but it was in God's eyes "a little while." God knew that the human heart longed for his presence. So in the fullness of time he sent his Son into a world dominated by tyranny and evil.

God sent his Son into the world to remove the shadow cast over all human activity by the original shame of Adam. The Son brought the light of life, that we might see our inherent dignity. He opened our deaf ears to God's word, that all men and women might know the way to dwell forever within the house of the Lord.

Today's Gospel describes the fallen condition of humanity and its remedy. Like the blind men, the human family senses its incompleteness. Under the heavy weight of sin, we long to have God stretch forth his hand and touch us. We yearn for the presence of someone who can actually respond to our urgent, desperate pleading and have pity. We don't need to see God clearly or know with certainty the Mystery he is. Being in his presence is enough.

And yet, when Jesus touched the eyes of the blind men, he made it clear that God had come to the human family as a presence that could be seen, heard, and touched. The presence of God is a tangible reality, one that longs to be known, experienced, and loved. God wants to be seen!

Through the sacraments of the Church and through her members, the presence of God in the Person of Jesus continues to be a substantial and incarnate reality. Through the power of the Holy Spirit, Abraham's redeemer continues to act in history, responding to the human need for perfect and unending love. Through the members of Christ's body, the God of the house of Jacob continues to wipe shame away and enlighten the eyes of his servants.

While awaiting the return of the Son of Man, the members of the Church must talk about Jesus all over the world. Others must see in our lives that the tyranny of sin has ended. They must receive from us an invitation to behold the "temple" of the Lord and an opportunity to savor his sweetness. They must sense in us the possibility of seeing themselves in a whole new way and of hearing the voice of the One who has never ceased calling out, "Where are you?"

Ah! how great is His mercy; I shall be able to sing of it only in heaven.

Saturday, Week One
  First Reading: Isaiah 30:19–21; 23–26
  Gospel: Matthew 9:35—10:5a, 6–8

Giving Without Charge

Today's Scripture passages make clear how we are expected to live between the first coming of Christ and his return in glory. Since he has already dressed our wounds and healed our hearts (Psalm 147), we must weep no more! By the gift of his life Christ has given us rain and bread, streams, watercourses, and wide pastures. We live now in Jerusalem, in the light of seven days as one. Whether we turn to the right or to the left, our ears should constantly hear from behind us, "This is the way; walk in it."

Should there be any doubt about the way we are to follow, Jesus describes it well. He tells the twelve that they are to "cure the sick, raise the dead, cleanse lepers, and drive out demons." The healing power of God is not a word, a slogan, or a message; it is an action! It is as real and as personal as the one who exercises it. This Word comes to us just as we are, so that through flesh and blood all people might know God's saving power.

In the Gospel Jesus has compassion for the harassed and dejected. He therefore establishes the means by which greater numbers of people will have access to his mercy. He empowers his apostles, and later he promises that all his followers will receive the same Holy Spirit (see John 16:7–14). Each will become an incarnate expression of his loving presence and respond in his name to the needs of others.

While the ordained and those in consecrated life undertake this in specific ways and for necessary purposes, every member of Christ's body has been called to cure, cleanse, and cast out. The harvest is indeed rich; thus the work of gathering it in belongs to the entire body of Christ. Through the members of the Church, Christ continues to make a tour through all the towns and villages of the world. Through us he continues to proclaim the Good News of the kingdom, to nourish, and to heal. While we await his return in glory, we are expected to be his hands and feet, his eyes and ears, but most especially his heart.

The scene recounted in the Gospel wonderfully and beautifully fulfills the words of the prophet Isaiah, for the Jerusalem of which he speaks is the kingdom of which Jesus preaches. Everyone baptized into Christ lives within this new and eternal city and is expected to bring all exiles back. As we await Christ's return, we are blessed to the extent that each of us, in his or her own way, cures, heals, binds up, casts out, and raises up.

I desire to accomplish Your will perfectly and to reach the degree of glory You have prepared for me in Your Kingdom.

Sunday, Week Two, Cycle A
  First Reading: Isaiah 11:1–10
  Second Reading: Romans 15:4–9
  Gospel: Matthew 3:1–12

It's Not Our Clothing

The season of Advent teaches us how to endure as we await the Lord's coming. It does so primarily by instilling in us "the encouragement of the Scriptures."

We know from the prophet Isaiah that the Lord will not judge "by appearance" nor decide "by hearsay," so we can look forward to his coming with hope. Jesus will "judge the poor with justice, and decide aright for the land's afflicted." When the Lord comes, there will be "no harm or ruin,… for the earth shall be filled with knowledge of the LORD."

When "John the Baptist appeared preaching in the desert of Judea," his purpose too was to encourage a return to the Lord. The people of the "whole region of the Jordan" went out to him, not to see a man clothed in camel's hair and eating "locusts and wild honey" but to receive the hope he preached. John's call was an invitation for people to turn their lives toward God and away from the world.

John knew that with the coming of Christ, people would be able to live in the world with a new perspective, that of the kingdom of God. John didn't want people to reject the world and live with him in the desert; he wanted them to center their lives on God so that they would recognize in Jesus how the promises made to the patriarchs were being fulfilled. John baptized with water, preparing the people for a baptism "with the Holy Spirit and with fire," which would enable their lives to manifest the truth of God. Paul encourages us to "think in harmony with one another" and "with one voice glorify the God and Father of our Lord Jesus Christ."

The Pharisees and Sadducees failed to comprehend. They came to John in fear, hoping to save themselves from God's wrath. They were not motivated by the desire for repentance, the urge to turn once again to God. They were hedging their bets against being "cut down and thrown into the fire." They were truly a "brood of vipers," an image of Satan and the other angels who refused to center their lives on God. These "vipers" exist forever in an "unquenchable fire" created by their refusal to see and accept reality within the context of serving God.

If, like St. Thérèse, we await Christ's coming with hope rooted in the Scriptures and with a confidence engendered by God's mercy, then we have nothing to fear. We can look forward to taking our place with the wolf and the lamb, the leopard and the kid, the calf and the young lion, for we are one with the "little child" who guides them "in fullness of peace forever" (Psalm 72:7).

Jesus does not demand great actions from us but simply surrender *and* gratitude.

Sunday, Week Two, Cycle B
  First Reading: Isaiah 40:1–5, 9–11
  Second Reading: 2 Peter 3:8–14
  Gospel: Mark 1:1–8

Patience and Peace

St. Peter reminds us exactly what we are awaiting: "new heavens and a new earth." This is not entirely different from that which John appeared in the desert proclaiming. His "baptism of repentance for the forgiveness of sins" opened people to the "mightier" one, whose baptism with the Holy Spirit would forever alter the way they saw God, themselves, others, and all of creation. John's message prepared the way for the comfort of expiated guilt of which the prophet Isaiah speaks. This "way of the Lord" means having our lives united with the life of God.

The words of today's First Reading give a descriptive overview of redemption both for the Israelites, exiled and captive, and for the entire human family. It is true that God "comes with power," but his strength is that of a shepherd. He longs to gather us all in his arms, hold us to his bosom, and lead us with care. In the new heavens and new earth that we await during the season of Advent, we will live forever within God's loving embrace.

This truth about the Lord's coming has not changed. God has not "delayed" in fulfilling the picture Isaiah describes, because, as St. Peter tells us, "one day is like a thousand years and a thousand years like one day." While we might consider it a delay, that is only because we do not yet see the unfolding of human history from the heights of Zion. From that vantage point we will see the straight and level path on which God always walks toward us and for us.

In order to prepare the way of the Lord, we must cry out at the top of our voice, heralding the good news that God wishes us all to "come to repentance" and wants none of us to perish. The Scriptures help us determine "what sort of persons" we ought to be here and now while we await the hereafter. We should be "eager to be without spot or blemish" and to be "at peace" at "the coming of the day of God."

St. Thérèse knew that the world could seem like a cultural and spiritual wilderness. But she also knew that, by the birth of Christ, God was now working in the world. Jesus was born so that human hearts could be transformed and the world could complete its journey.

Thérèse believed that love was the surest sign of the human heart's conversion. She experienced this for herself on Christmas Day when she was thirteen years of age. From that point on, she stood on the heights of Zion and expressed her relationship with Christ through love.

Ah! how true it is that God alone knows human hearts.

Sunday, Week Two, Cycle C
First Reading: Baruch 5:1–9
Second Reading: Philippians 1:4–6, 8–11
Gospel: Luke 3:1–6

Taking a Stand

The First Reading vividly describes the stance of the Christian during the season of Advent. Recalling the words that foretold the first coming of Christ should fill us with joy. In him we have taken off the "robe of mourning and misery" that came from sin. Through baptism we have put on "the cloak of justice from God," and our heads bear "the glory of the eternal name." Thus we can "stand upon the heights," looking ahead to that time when God will gather his children "from the east and the west,… borne aloft on royal thrones."

Paul then reminds us that "the one who began the good work in us" will complete it. Thus we advance in our lives of faith. We know that in Christ God remembers us!

The Word of God should burst forth from each of us, just as it did from "John the son of Zechariah." Knowing where and how we stand should incite us to "prepare the way of the Lord" and "make straight his paths." If we allow Jesus to lead us "by the light of his glory," then through us "all flesh shall see the salvation of God."

Although the names Tiberius Caesar, Herod, Annas, Caiaphas, and Pontius Pilate have changed, Christianity remains entrenched in history through the members of Christ's body. Once we were all "captives," but through the forgiveness of our sins we are filled with the "fruit of righteousness." Therefore we share a partnership in the Gospel, one that demands of us the willingness to go throughout "the whole region" of our lives so that love may increase more and more. This is how the nations of the world will know that, in the words of today's psalm, "the Lord has done great things for them" (Psalm 126:2).

St. Thérèse knew where she stood! Her confidence in God's love filled her heart "with the affection of Christ Jesus" of which St. Paul speaks to the Philippians. Although confined by cloister walls, she was able to make God's salvation known to the entire world. She discerned the great value of doing everything with great love. She made the "rough ways...smooth" by embracing every sacrifice as if she were embracing the cross of Christ.

Thérèse knew that Christ came to save her and that "his mercy and justice" were her company. With her let us remember where we stand and why Christ was born. Then we can be "filled with the fruit of righteousness that comes through Jesus Christ for the glory and praise of God."

This same Spirit of Love also says: "For to him that is little, mercy will be shown."

December 12: The Feast of Our Lady of Guadalupe
First Reading: Zechariah 2:14–17
Alternative: Revelation 11:19a; 12:1–6a, 10ab
Gospel: Luke 1:26–38
Alternative: Luke 1:39–47

The Great Sign
Since the apparition of Our Lady of Guadalupe in 1531, "many nations [have joined] themselves to the LORD." Mary appeared to one of the indigenous peoples of Mexico as a great sign that, through the child conceived in her womb, God wished to dwell among all peoples of the world. The gift of redemption is not for an elect few but for all women and men.

The Lord of hosts sent Mary to tell these peoples that "salvation and power," "the Kingdom of our God," and the "authority of his Anointed" have come to them. Mary let them know, in her own words, that she is their most merciful mother, that they are as much her children as is the son she bore. To this day the Mexican people continue to accept her maternal care.

The woman "clothed with the sun, with the moon under her feet," appeared like one of the people to whom she was sent. Her image, fixed for ages on the tilma of Juan Diego, bears witness to the fact that the Son of God is fully human. The Lord comes to us as we are, with the desire to restore us to the dignity of his image and likeness.

The apparition of Our Lady of Guadalupe can also be described as another occasion when Mary set out "in haste" to celebrate the good news of God's redemptive love. Her maternal presence and the words she spoke have instilled in the heart of a nation the truth that God loves and cares for them. Salvation is not an impersonal act undertaken by a disinterested God. It is as intimately personal as the unexpected conceptions of two children—one in the womb of a young virgin and one in the womb of an aged woman "thought to be barren."

"The dragon [that] stood before the woman," waiting to "devour her child," was not driven away by heroic human strength but by the simple words a maiden spoke to an angel, "May it be done to me according to your word." We should not fear the coming of her Son in glory. Rather we should believe that everything the Lord has spoken will be fulfilled.

The season of Advent is a time to recall why Jesus came: so that we can look forward to an unimpeded experience of his presence, an eternity of loving communion purified of all imperfection, weakness, and sin. As long as we accept, with the people of Mexico, that Mary is our most merciful mother and that her Son occupies "the throne of David his father," then our souls, like hers, will proclaim "the greatness of the Lord." And "nothing will be impossible for God."

My one purpose, then, would be to accomplish the will of God, to sacrifice myself for Him in the way that would please Him.

Monday, Week Two
  First Reading: Isaiah 35:1–10
  Gospel: Luke 5:17–26

Which Is Easier?

Looking at the words of the prophet Isaiah, we might be inclined to think of his description of how things will be for "those whom the LORD has ransomed" as metaphor. Burning sands can no more become pools and thirsty ground springs of water than can a paralytic "rise and walk." And yet that is exactly what happens in today's Gospel. Luke recounts for us just what Isaiah prophesied, for in the healing of the paralytic, the knees of the weak are in fact made firm!

We must never overlook the fact that Isaiah's depiction of redemption embraces the whole created order. He has left us a vivid and wholly positive portrayal of the highway God will provide in our journey toward him. The prophet's words should foster within each one of us confidence in this holy Way, especially as we know this Way personally and by name.

The friends of the paralytic walk upon the highway Isaiah foretold. They know that there is only one hope for the blind and the deaf and the paralytic: being in the presence of Jesus. Their confidence should purge from our hearts and minds all contemptuous cynicism and petulant doubt. Their bold initiative should strengthen our feeble hands and cast out any fear.

The power of the Lord for healing assumed flesh and blood through Mary, precisely that we might know how easy it is for God to say, "Your sins are forgiven!" This is not blasphemy. This is the truth to which Jesus came to testify in order that we might know the ease with which God the Father dispenses love.

The healing power of the Lord has not left the world. Through the Church the presence of the Lord saturates human history in such a way that people everywhere can say, "We have seen incredible things!" It is our responsibility to enable the tongues of the mute to sing, because we know the longing in human hearts and the Way to set them free. Having ourselves been told to rise, we should glorify God by dispensing the same love that first enabled us to stand up from our fallen condition.

On the highway Jesus has laid out for us, there are no beasts of prey. By his birth we are crowned with everlasting joy. Sorrow and mourning have truly fled, because God has lifted the yoke of our captivity. In the coming of his only begotten Son, we are saved.

Coming into this land of exile, You willed to suffer and to die in order to draw souls to the bosom of the Eternal Fire of the Blessed Trinity.

Tuesday, Week Two
  First Reading: Isaiah 40:1–11
  Gospel: Matthew 18:12–14

What Shall I Cry Out?

The words of the prophet Isaiah should naturally draw our attention to that greatest of all desert figures, John the Baptist. Crying out at the top of his voice, he prepared the way for the Lord among a multitude of people, including even the scribes and Pharisees. John was not afraid to say to the cities of Judah, "Here is your God…. Here is his reward with him!" In his day John fulfilled the prophet's command to proclaim to the people that their "service is at an end." And so must we in our own day.

The reason people came to listen to the man dressed in camel's hair and eating locusts and wild honey is that they needed hope! They did not go into the desert to be excoriated for their misdeeds; they were aware of their weaknesses and failures. They longed to be liberated from the guilt that weighed them down. They longed to be more loving, more caring, more sensitive, more attentive and responsive to God.

John offered them the comfort described at the beginning of today's First Reading. He spoke "tenderly" to the multitudes, because he knew that God longed to gather his people "in his arms…carrying them close in his bosom, and leading [them] with care." John knew that the Lord was truly "like a shepherd."

When John points out Jesus as the Lamb of God, he asserts God's solidarity with the human family. God's power is revealed in the willingness of his only begotten Son to become one like us—a "sheep"—in all things but sin. This is the ultimate expression of God's love.

How beautifully then does today's Gospel recount for us the truth of God's power! The Father wants not one of his little ones to be lost. In his Son he has taken up a place with us, precisely to search out those lost in the dark valleys of human fragility and the wastelands of human indifference. Jesus's words should therefore give us comfort and strengthen our hope, for sometimes we still wander.

The prophet's command is the unique responsibility of those whom Christ has lifted up through the waters of baptism and returned to the fold of his Body. We must unite our voices with St. John and continue with tenderness to cry out at the top of our voices, "Here comes with power the Lord GOD."

In spite of my extreme littleness I still dare to gaze upon the Divine Sun, the Sun of Love, and my heart feels within it all the aspirations of an Eagle.

Wednesday, Week Two
First Reading: Isaiah 40:25–31
Gospel: Matthew 11:28–30

Resting From Sin

Sin, besides being boring, is exhausting. It is the reason "young men faint and grow weary, and youths stagger and fall." Sin drains the vigor and vitality of our humanity, weakening our hope. Sin imposes an oppressive burden that no human being can lift. Only the "eternal God" can "renew [our] strength."

This was the message of the prophet Isaiah. Speaking to a people worn down by their own transgressions, Isaiah offered hope. The Lord would not deal with them according to their crimes, but rather, by "his great might and the strength of his power," he would "redeem [them] from destruction," as Psalm 103 tells us, and crown them "with kindness and compassion."

The crown in today's psalm is also the "yoke" Jesus extends to the crowds in today's Gospel. It is one we received on the day we were baptized. After coming up out of the water, we took this yoke upon ourselves by being "crowned" with sacred chrism, in order that we might share in the priestly, prophetic, and kingly life of Christ. By this holy anointing hope has been restored, and we are able to "soar as with eagle's wings" on the winds of the Spirit, as he guides us through life, directing our thoughts and actions. Freed from the burden of sin, we readily take upon ourselves the burden of loving others just as the Lord loves us, with the gifts the Spirit gives to assist in the saving ministry.

Isaiah's words to the people were not about God bringing an end to an historical situation. They aimed at setting the sights of the people on something far greater, the day when the graciousness and mercy of God would be definitively revealed. Isaiah wanted the people to know that there would indeed come a time when they would "run and not grow weary, walk and not grow faint."

The crowds coming to Jesus surely recognized in his words an echo of Isaiah's prophecy. Jesus was inviting them to enter into that rest that was forfeited when Adam and Eve disobeyed God and took upon themselves the laborious burden of sin. Since that moment we have struggled to once again be at rest with God, to see the One "who has created these things," and to see all these things with God's eyes.

In today's Gospel, grace comes to the crowd just as it has come to us, in the Person of Christ. Through him God has responded to the fear that our ways are "hidden from the LORD" and that he has "disregarded" us. In Jesus we are able to find our strength in the One who does not faint or grow weary and whose knowledge is beyond scrutiny. In Jesus our iniquities have been pardoned and our ills have been healed. We have only to accept his invitation to bless his holy name.

My folly *consists in begging the eagles, my brothers, to obtain for me the favor of flying towards the Sun of Love.*

Thursday, Week Two
First Reading: Isaiah 41:13–20
Gospel: Matthew 11:11–15

The Least Is the Greatest

The Church uses Isaiah's words to help prepare us for the coming of Christ in glory, just as Isaiah used them to prepare the Israelites for the coming of Christ in time. Prayerfully reflecting on Isaiah's inspiring imagery helps deepen our understanding of the Person of Christ, such that we can "rejoice in the LORD" on the occasion of his birth and "fear not" over the prospect of his return.

The One who came in time to "open up rivers on the bare heights, and fountains in the broad valleys" will make clear on his return that God has always answered "the afflicted and the needy." While there may indeed be times we feel like a "worm" or a "maggot," God will always help us, for he is our redeemer. When Jesus returns in glory, all will "see and know, observe and understand" that God has never forsaken us. God will make of us a "threshing sledge" to crush the obstacles that prevent us from experiencing the abundance of his love.

Today's psalm reminds us that the kingdom we await is "a kingdom for all ages" (Psalm 145:13). What began with the birth of Jesus in Nazareth was not just for the people of Israel but for "all generations." God has not forsaken the human family; rather, through the blood of Christ, he has more than satisfied us. No longer do we seek water in vain; the arid ground of our souls has welled up with springs of everlasting life.

Even those who are "least in the Kingdom of heaven" know this. Having heard the words of Christ, they open their lives to "all the prophets and the law prophesied." Through water and the

Holy Spirit, they are born again, not of women but through grace, such that the kindness and mercy of God have placed them on a height exceeding that of John the Baptist. And like John the Baptist, they cry into the desert-life of sin, inviting others to come and know the glorious splendor of God's kingdom.

As we prepare to celebrate Christ's birth and as we await his return in glory, we are called to make known God's might, not through force or with violence but by faithfulness and with gratitude. By the "hand of the LORD" we have been saved through the union of our lives with that of Christ. We should trust in the status of our rebirth and herald the coming of our God and King.

Never have I felt before this, dear Mother, how sweet and merciful the Lord really is.

Friday, Week Two
First Reading: Isaiah 48:17–19
Gospel: Matthew 11:16–19

Prosperity Through Obedience

The comparison Jesus makes in today's Gospel makes it clear that, between his coming to us as man and his return in glory, whimsy should not determine our lives. Following Jesus, "the Holy One of Israel," entails the willingness to dance or mourn, eat or drink, always at the appropriate time. We learn the tune that's being played and the song that's being sung from the "light of life" shining upon our own. By letting the Lord "lead [us] on the way [we] should go," we learn "what is for [our] good" and discover how obedience to the commandments leads to prosperity.

This "prosperity," long described by the Church as human flourishing, has little to do with social standing or economic security. Rather it is the continuing development of the goods and the virtues that are most perfective of human life. Following Christ, therefore, is an ongoing education in the truth of our humanity. We learn from him to "meditate on [God's] law day and night," as Psalm 1 tells us today. Thus we acquire the wisdom that helps us withstand the "counsel of the wicked," the false and arbitrary judgments of our generation.

Following our Redeemer ensures that we will be planted firmly where we are meant to be: by the "running water" of everlasting life. There is no need to pursue what cannot satisfy. Once we feast upon the food of heaven and drink the inebriating Blood of Christ, our identities become secure in the relationship that perfectly defines them: our relationship with God—Father, Son, and Holy Spirit.

The "Holy One of Israel" came to sustain our lives with his mercy. Our willingness to follow the paths that Jesus marks out for us makes our lives concrete vindications of his own. We who have been baptized into Christ's life become the glorious works of his wisdom. Our names will never be "blotted out" from God's presence.

Thus, as we follow Jesus now, we look forward in hope to that dwelling place in heaven that Christ has gained for us (see 2 Corinthians 5:2). Through our obedience to all he teaches us, we celebrate his birth not as an anecdote of the past but as the sure and steady satisfaction of our hearts' deepest hunger.

I have no trouble in carrying the burden of obedience.

Saturday, Week Two
   First Reading: Sirach 48:1–4. 9–11
   Gospel: Matthew 17:9a, 10–13

The Fire of Love

The advent of Christ begins with the birth of John the Baptist (see Luke 1:5–24). At the beginning of his "orderly sequence of events," St. Luke establishes a bond uniting the life of John with that of his cousin Jesus. This authoritatively confirms the fact that John is more than just an incidental part of the Christian narrative. This is the point Jesus makes in today's Gospel when describing John in relation to the prophet Elijah.

The comparison to which Jesus draws the apostles' attention was also made at the announcement of John's birth. The angel Gabriel calmed Zechariah's fears by describing the child yet to be born as one who would "turn the hearts of fathers toward children" (Luke 1:17). As a member of the priestly class, the meaning of this was certainly not lost on Zechariah. Perhaps it was the reason for his initial incredulity.

For the past few days, Sacred Scripture, like Gabriel and Jesus, has been pointing to the figure of John. Today's reading from the book of Sirach, although descriptive of Elijah, also urges us to recognize John, praise his "wondrous deeds," and seek his "friendship."

The glory of Elijah—his appearance, words, actions, and departure, including the horses that carried him aloft—is depicted with the word *fire*. This bold imagery underscores how Elijah's life was charged with the presence of God. Like the bush Moses encountered in the desert (see Exodus 3), his life was aflame with the love of God but never destroyed by it. It was this loving presence that enabled Elijah to "shut up the heavens," perform "wondrous deeds," "reestablish the tribes of Jacob," and "put an end to wrath before the day of the LORD." This fire of God's love was the force to "turn back the hearts of fathers toward their sons." It was the source of the blessing on all who fell asleep in his friendship.

The "fire" of Elijah explains why so many were attracted to the person of John the Baptist. John's "words were as a flaming furnace," which singed the hearts of those who came out to him in the desert and turned them to the Lord. This would open them to seeing God's face in the person of Jesus. God sent John to "protect what [his] right hand had planted" (Psalm 80:16) by opening people to the new life that would come through Jesus's baptism "of the Holy Spirit and with fire" (Luke 3:16).

The inextricable bond John shares with Jesus is no different from the one Jesus longs to share with us. It is a bond of friendship forged in the fire of divine love.

I understand so well that it is only love which makes us acceptable to God, that this love is the only good ambition.

Sunday, Week Three, Cycle A
First Reading: Isaiah 35:1–6, 10
Second Reading: James 5:7–10
Gospel: Matthew 11:2–11

Waiting in Patience

At times it is difficult to "be patient…until the coming of the Lord." The conditions of life can frighten our hearts. We might feel that our knees are indeed "weak," and our hands "feeble." Spiritual struggles may leave our souls thirsting for the "early and late rains" of which St. James speaks in today's Second Reading. Often we can sum up our complaints in the question the disciples of St. John the Baptist ask Jesus, "Are you the one who is to come?"

The season of Advent particularly suits every heart weakened from waiting "for the precious fruit of the earth" with respect to family, health, security, and love. We learn from Jesus how the words of Isaiah can focus our attention on everything we have heard and seen with respect to the God who comes to save us. We are reminded that even "the least born into the kingdom of heaven" is greater than John the Baptist, because such a one is no longer blind to God's vision or deaf to his voice. We are cleansed of the leprosy of sin, which prevented us from drawing close to God.

The Scriptures chosen for this season should make our hearts firm. They are filled with words from prophets who waited patiently to see what we have seen. They recall for us the fact that God has indeed fulfilled his promises. Christ raises up "all that were bowed down" (Psalm 146:8). Those who hungered for God are now fed by the Body and Blood of his Son. Those who felt alone are now sustained by his abiding presence. Those who longed to stand against the oppression of the wicked have been strengthened.

The Lord has ransomed us! Whatever doubts well up within, whatever sorrow and mourning encroach upon our joy, the fact is that "the Lord keeps faith forever" (Psalm 146:6). God has planted his life within us. We must be like farmers waiting for the abundant bloom that will signify the glory of his return. The Lord crowns with everlasting joy "the one who takes no offense at him."

St. Thérèse went into the desert of Carmel to see the Lord more clearly. There in the confines of the cloister, "the glory of Lebanon" was given her. She learned the truth of everything "the prophets…spoke in the name of the Lord," not through bold visions and mystical insights but through physical and spiritual suffering. She knew that the Lord is always close at hand to those who feel frightened or feeble.

I have only to cast a glance in the Gospels and immediately I breathe in the perfumes of Jesus's life, and I know on which side to run.

Sunday, Week Three, Cycle B
First Reading: Isaiah 61:1–2, 10–11
Second Reading: 1 Thessalonians 5:16–24
Gospel: John 1:6–8, 19–28

The Joy of Our Souls

We can learn many things from "Bethany across the Jordan." The first thing we can learn is that the Lord's coming has always been prepared by "glad tidings." The prophet Isaiah understood this just as surely as did John the Baptist.

Although John was reluctant to place himself in such company, the anointing he received was a cause of great joy, even from his mother's womb (see Luke 1:44). God entrusted Isaiah, John, and all the prophets with a message of hope and healing for the poor, the brokenhearted, the imprisoned, and captives. Each one in his time willingly announced "a day of vindication by our God," "a year of favor," a never-ending experience of a light that could penetrate the darkness of our weak, fractured, and vulnerable humanity. All the prophets could "rejoice heartily in the Lord" and "refrain from every kind of evil," so as not to "quench the Spirit" that had been given them.

Thus we come to a second lesson from Bethany across the Jordan: We learn that we cannot heal ourselves. God alone fills the hungry with good things, scatters the proud in their conceit, casts down the mighty from their thrones, and lifts up the lowly (see Luke 1:46–55). God accomplishes all this from within us, because he holds the keys to the deepest places of our hearts. The transformation he effects depends upon our willingness to do as St. Paul tells the Thessalonians, to pray constantly. Through an ongoing interior conversation with God, our lives unceasingly "testify to the light," and we become—like Isaiah, Elijah, and John the Baptist—voices crying out to others how to "make straight the way of the Lord."

This leads us to a third lesson from Bethany across the Jordan: It is the God of peace who makes us holy! The message of the prophets frees us from the enslaving burden of having to justify ourselves before God. Now we truly can rejoice in all circumstances, because God has "clothed [us] in a robe of salvation and wrapped [us] in a mantle of justice." As long as we do not "despise prophetic utterances" and reject the guidance that comes from the Spirit, we will certainly know what is for our good.

St. Thérèse lived her entire life "in Bethany across the Jordan." She entered Carmel knowing very well what she went "out to the desert to see," the light to which John gave testimony (Matthew 11:8). Thus her life became prophetic. Knowing that she was too little to untie Jesus's sandal strap, she let him untie hers and then wash her feet. God became the joy of her soul, and she became God's bride, bedecked with the greatest of all jewels, a life of constant thankfulness.

I also felt the desire of loving only God, of finding my joy only in Him.

Sunday, Week Three, Cycle C
First Reading: Zephaniah 3:14–18a
Second Reading: Philippians 4:4–7
Gospel: Luke 3:10–18

The Cause of Our Joy

Those of us living between the first coming of Christ and his return in glory should find it easy to "shout for joy." We know that "God is in [our] midst," because Jesus, our "mighty savior," has renewed us in God's love. Jesus, by his passion, death, and resurrection, has "turned away" our great enemy, Satan, and exposed the ordinary circumstances of our lives to that peace "that surpasses all understanding." Knowing that the Lord is ever near to us and "has removed the judgment" against us should banish all our fears.

This, essentially, is the good news John the Baptist preached to the crowds that came out to him in the desert. John filled them with expectation, as his words and actions touched the deepest desires of their hearts. His preaching prepared their lives for a fire that would expel anxiety, greed, extortion, and all other dispositions and behaviors that restrict human relationships and diminish bonds of trust. John told them how to respond to the common, ordinary demands of real life with a joy and confidence secured in the knowledge that the Lord is ever near.

We too have no "further misfortunes" to fear, because we have been baptized "with the Holy Spirit and fire." Therefore we should be confident and unafraid. As we prepare to celebrate Christ's birth, we do so knowing that one day we will experience fully the presence of the "mightier" one, the God who is our

Savior. We know that when Christ comes with his "winnowing fan," he will clear the chaff from our lives and gather us into the fullness of the life and love that is our destiny.

Truly does "the Lord rejoice over us." Like the crowds to whom John preached, this truth should ultimately determine every aspect of our lives. It should mark us with a kindness that touches everyone we encounter. No matter the situation or the circumstance, we must be "confident and unafraid" (Isaiah 12:2, Psalm Response), a people of joy whose courage and strength come from the Spirit of the Lord who is upon us.

Like those questioning John in today's Gospel, St. Thérèse of Lisieux asked the Lord, "What must I do?" In the words of St. Paul she found the answer to her question: "The way which surpasses all the others…love" (1 Corinthians 13:1). She realized that her vocation was to be "love in the heart of the Church." From that moment on she had no anxiety whatsoever.

The "peace of God that surpasses all understanding" guided Thérèse's heart and opened her mind to instruction from Christ Jesus. She knew an ever-growing expectation that Christ would fulfill every longing in her heart and not delay in taking her to himself. This expectation became the cause of her joy.

[M]y vocation, at last I have found it…MY VOCATION IS LOVE!

Monday, Week Three
First Reading: Numbers 24:2–7, 15–17a
Gospel: Matthew: 21:23–27

We, Too, Can Raise Our Eyes

Like Balaam, each one of us can "raise [our] eyes" and utter the words God longs for people to hear. His oracle reaches well beyond the encampments of Israel. It makes its way into every human heart, because every heart instinctively yearns to know the ways of the Lord and be instructed in his paths.

The "star [that] advances from Jacob" signals an event that will transcend the Israelites' hopes for restoration and renewal. It points to the star that will come to rest over the place where Jesus lies in the manger. That star is a lasting sign that all men and women can "hear what God says," "know what the Most High knows," and "see what the Almighty sees, enraptured and with eyes unveiled."

The chief priests and elders of the people question the authority of Jesus because his methods contradict theirs. Jesus's words and actions focus on the compassion, kindness, and mercy of God, while the chief priests and the elders rely on manipulation and control. In the temple area this day, they sense that they are losing people to Jesus, just as they lost them to John.

The season of Advent seeks to remind us that the Lord is "good and upright, thus he shows sinners the way" and "guides the humble" (Psalm Response, Psalm 25:8–9). In a short time we will celebrate the fact that God has come to us as and where we are, so that we can be with him now and forever. The birth of the Son fulfills God's longing to speak to us as one friend speaks to another (see Exodus 33:11).

The season of Advent reminds us that Christ has removed the veil that prevented us from seeing the truth. Now we can set out on his paths. We can avoid the path of destruction that results from following our own ways.

The oracle of Balaam is as timely now as when first uttered. The world today needs to hear the claim that God has visited his people and has pitched his tent among us. The world needs to hear that walking humbly with God is as simple as honestly admitting that goodness and beauty, justice and truth, are greater than what we can conceive, manufacture, or sustain. The oracle of Balaam springs from the knowledge that God is good and upright, that his wells yield free-flowing waters, that his Son's reign is greater than that of any earthly ruler or form of government, and that his royalty is exalted in the lives of his people.

Since Jesus has reascended into heaven, I can follow Him only in the traces He has left; but how luminous these traces are!

Tuesday, Week Three
  First Reading: Zephaniah 3:1–2, 9–13
  Gospel: Matthew 21:28–32

The Work of the Vineyard

Rather than focus on the people mentioned in today's Gospel, we should ask ourselves first: What is the work the father wants his sons to "go out" and do? Jesus often uses the word *vineyard* as a metaphor for the kingdom of God, so we should be clear on just what it means to work there. Only then can we appreciate why tax collectors and sinners could "not be ashamed of all [their] deeds" and "rebellious actions" and were entering God's kingdom before the chief priests and the elders of the people.

In today's First Reading the prophet Zephaniah describes the work of the vineyard as an act of change and purification. What is "rebellious and polluted" and "tyrannical" becomes "humble and lowly." God cleanses the lips of his people, so that they can call upon his name and "serve him with one accord."

The work that God undertakes on behalf of a people who no longer trust in or listen to him is an act of love. God longs to have his people near him; thus he will remove from their midst whatever has distracted them. As a result they will be able to "pasture and couch their flocks with none to disturb them."

This is the same message John preaches. Tax collectors and prostitutes are responding to it because they hear an answer to the cries of their crushed spirits and broken hearts. John offers them a new way of life. Their former way of life has kept them from drawing near to the Lord; now God is drawing near to them. Through the words of John and in the waters of his baptism, they can look to the Lord, radiant with joy.

The chief priests and elders of the people are unwilling to heed John's voice and accept correction. They reject his way of righteousness because they can't accept the notion that God's love reaches "beyond the rivers of Ethiopia and as far as the recesses of the North." Eventually they will reject outright John and his cousin, the one whose life definitively reveals God's love. Jesus wants to change their minds. His message is that it is never too late "to go out and work in the vineyard." It is never too late to love others the way that God loves us.

While we await the full and unending experience of God drawing near to us, we must continue to work in the vineyard. We must continue to make God's love real in every condition and circumstance of our lives. We must bear God's righteousness through word and deed, so that others will believe and enter in, and the kingdom may grow. The greatest offering we can bring to the Lord is to continue working in his vineyard.

I understood above all that charity must not remain hidden in the bottom of the heart.

Wednesday, Week Three
  First Reading: Isaiah 45:6c–8, 18, 21c–25
  Gospel: Luke 7:18b–23

The One We Look For

The prophet Isaiah spoke to a people who had turned away from God, "the designer and maker of the earth." As the Israelites grew into a nation, they gradually began to "look for another." They adopted religious attitudes and social practices that would eventually leave them spiritually blind, lame, deaf, poor, and leprous.

Isaiah's words encouraged them to repent, to turn back to the "just and saving God" and adhere to his "unalterable word" in humility and worship. These hopeful words looked forward to a time when "justice [would] descend [from the] heavens" and "salvation bud forth."

John the Baptist was also a messenger of hope. He spent his life preparing people for the unimagined way in which God would reveal "the vindication and the glory of all the descendants of Israel." Now sensing that God's salvation is near, he sends his disciples to Jesus, whose every word and every action resonate with John's knowledge of God's promises.

Jesus, knowing full well what John is asking, confirms what John has long suspected: "The blind regain their sight, the lame walk, lepers are cleansed, the deaf hear, the dead are raised, and the poor have the good news proclaimed to them."

The circumstances of life today can push us to "look for another." We understandably long for someone or something that can cure every disease, alleviate human suffering, and drive away evil spirits. Yet Jesus's death for the forgiveness of sin is the greatest of his miracles. Rejecting this gift is the offense to which Jesus makes reference at the end of the Gospel passage.

During the season of Advent, we are reminded why the earth brought forth a savior. Jesus came into the world to make the human heart new, thereby bringing together kindness and truth, justice and peace, in the lives and actions of those set free from sin. Through the gift of the Spirit, the Lord fills us with "his benefits" (Psalm Response, Psalm 85:13), which he gives to enlighten, strengthen, and transform us. This great season recalls for us the vital truth that our lives are not a waste, that we were created "from of old" to live within the one and only God.

We should listen then to what the Lord has to say. For

> Justice shall walk before him,
>> and salvation, along the way of his steps. (Psalm 85:14)

I had the happiness of contemplating for a long time the marvels Jesus is working.

Thursday, Week Three
  First Reading: Isaiah 54:1–10
  Gospel: Luke 7:24–30

Accepting God's Plan

Throughout the season of Advent, the Lord reminds us of his promise to Noah that the waters of the flood would "never again deluge the earth." Each day the Scriptures attest to the fact that God is not angry with us and has not rebuked us. What could be better than hearing God say to us, "My love shall never leave you nor my covenant of peace be shaken"? These words should penetrate the depths of our hearts and be the foundation of our lives. This is God's plan for us.

In today's Gospel Jesus points out how the Pharisees and scholars of the law have rejected God's plan. John was sent to "prepare [the] way," but they could not accept that it was open to everyone, even tax collectors and sinners. They refused to "enlarge the space for [their] tent" and "spread out [their] cloths unsparingly." Although John was the greatest "among those born of women," that's not what the Pharisees and scholars went out to the desert to see.

The time between the first and second comings of Christ can seem like a desert. Like the crowds in today's Gospel, we also need to be reminded of the "numerous...children" born of water and the Holy Spirit. We need to hear through Jesus how the "God of all the earth" has called us back to himself with an enduring love. Even the least of us, Jesus says, is greater than John! We are no longer disgraced, because God has "brought [us] from the nether world" and given us a place in his kingdom.

The ordinary burdens of life make it easy to lose sight of this. Yet the sufferings we experience, the frustrations we have, and even the doubts that call into question what we have seen with the eyes of faith can never fully overshadow the tenderness of God. The times when we feel as if God has abandoned us and hidden his face are but "brief moments" in his eternal plan.

God forgets even "the shame of [our] youth." In the most difficult, trying, and confusing moments of life, he draws near to us. This was the message John preached; this was the message that led the people who listened to him to accept baptism.

The season of Advent presents in a new way the question Jesus proposes to the crowd. What do we expect from God? What do we go to Church expecting to receive?

Those who accepted John's baptism believed that their lives could be filled with the righteousness of God. They believed that even if "the mountains" were to "leave their place," God would never leave them. They believed that the Lord could change their mourning into dancing. Thus they welcomed God's plan.

Our faults could not cause God any pain, and this assurance filled me with joy, helping me to bear patiently with life's exile.

Friday, Week Three
  First Reading: Isaiah 56:1–3a, 6–8
  Gospel: John 5:33–36

Testifying to the Truth

Through Sacred Scripture the Church presents us with two important emissaries during this holy season: the prophet Isaiah and St. John the Baptist. For the past few days, not only have the words of the first overlapped with the message of the second, but we have learned of the fulfillment of their words in the ministry of Jesus. This is intentional.

The Church uses the words of these men and the deeds of Jesus as "a burning and shining lamp" by which the past becomes the way of the present and the future. In other words, looking backward teaches us about what lies ahead. Truly grasping Christ's coming in glory affects how we live here and now. When we realize that God's "salvation is about to come," we want to "observe what is right, do what is just," "keep the sabbath free from profanation," and restrain our hands "from any evildoing." Everything we learn from Scripture should make us fear the Lord but not be afraid of his coming (see Psalm Response, Psalm 67).

Each passage we have heard from the prophet Isaiah has testified to the truth of how God would redeem and restore his people. The prophet's words in today's reading certainly shattered the expectations of the people in his time. It was unthinkable that "foreigners [could] join themselves to the LORD" or that God's house would "be called a house of prayer for all peoples." But only by accepting the prophet's words about what was to come could the people begin to experience the shining light of God's countenance and the joy of being on his holy mountain.

John teaches us that God's plan to gather all nations to himself began with the advent of his Son. In the Person of Jesus of Nazareth, God's salvation has been revealed to the nations. John testified to the truth of Isaiah's words by preparing people for and then leading them to Jesus. If they could accept the fact that the promise of the past was being fulfilled in the present, they could experience the saving power of God's love. The incarnation, life, death, and resurrection of Jesus would be a testimony far greater than John's.

We need to look at the first coming of Christ and the works that he performed in order to be clear about his return. If those works convince us that the Father sent him, we will yearn for Christ's return in the hope of a full and unending experience of the Father's love. If we can see in the works of Christ that the Father rules all peoples with equity, we will be emboldened to keep his covenant now. If we have confidence in the Father's mercy, our lives will likewise testify to the truth that the Father sent the Son to join all peoples to himself. And this is reason enough to await his return.

Jesus, O Jesus, if the desire of loving You is so delightful, what will it be to possess and enjoy this Love?

★ ★ ★

NOTE: For the Saturday of this week, see the appropriate date in the following pages.

Sunday, Week Four, Cycle A
  First Reading: Isaiah 7:10–14
  Second Reading: Romans 1:1–7
  Gospel: Matthew 1:18–24

God's Time

We should not consider Ahaz's response in today's First Reading insolent. Despite his being commanded by God to ask for a fitting sign for the unfolding of his redemptive plan, Ahaz was wise enough to know the limits of human wisdom. No one could have predicted the way in which "the king of glory" would enter into the world (Psalm Response, Psalm 24).

Instead of punishing or rebuking Ahaz, God offered his own sign, one that would puzzle and trouble the leaders of his people for centuries. Who would this virgin or young woman be? What did it mean that her child would be called Emmanuel?

By the time Mary and Joseph were betrothed, there were many different positions about the meaning of Isaiah's words. It would be absurd to suppose that Joseph should have known that his betrothed was the virgin of the prophecy. God is the only one who could make sense of the events that were quietly unfolding in Joseph and Mary's life. God is the only one who could restore a sense of "grace…and peace" to this righteous man who was "unwilling to expose [Mary] to shame."

Through the calm of sleep, God extends to Joseph "the grace of apostleship," and Joseph awakens ready to do what has been commanded. By accepting the words of the angel regarding the conception of Mary's child, Joseph will, in his own way, "bring about the obedience of faith" of which St. Paul speaks in the Second Reading. By taking Mary and the child into his care,

Joseph will do his part in seeing that the child "descended from David according to the flesh" will be "established as Son of God in power."

Matthew's story of the birth of Jesus Christ begins without ordeal. There is no mention of a dramatic announcement by Mary concerning the mysterious and wordless overshadowing of her life by the Holy Spirit. Although Joseph initially intends to divorce Mary quietly, he welcomes her into his home. The depiction of these events seems so commonplace that Matthew has to remind us about the sign God gave to Ahaz. Through the lives of Mary and Joseph, "what the Lord had said through the prophets" is fulfilled.

God's plan will continue to unfold without ordeal and according to his time line. There is no rush, no hurry, and no commotion—just two people living their lives together and with God. While Ahaz reminds us that we should not ask or demand a sign from God, Mary and Joseph remind us that God's plan unfolds in the common and ordinary circumstances of our lives. Through the obedience of faith, the "king of glory" enters into our lives without force or violence, calling us to be holy and reminding us always that God is with us.

St. Thérèse is best known for her little way of spiritual childhood. Like Joseph and Mary, she understood that God's ways and his timing are not our own. She knew that even the littlest and most insignificant part of her life could express her apostleship and further the expansion of God's kingdom. All she needed was to trust that in all things God was with her, helping her live her vocation "for the Gospel of God."

The way of simple love and confidence is really made for you.

Sunday, Week Four, Cycle B
  First Reading: 2 Samuel 7:1–5, 8b–12, 14a–16
  Second Reading: Romans 16:25–27
  Gospel 1:26–38

Troubled by God

The season of Advent is meant to trouble us, in the same way Mary was "troubled" at the greeting of the angel Gabriel. The imagery of the prophet Isaiah, the emphasis on the figure of John the Baptist, and Nathan's words to David in the First Reading have been carefully selected to grab our attention and fix it upon the inconceivable way in which the "prophetic writings" have been fulfilled.

This is especially true with respect to today's Gospel passage. St. Luke's narrative describes the raising up of an heir of King David in a manner that is wholly incredulous! The child who will be given "the throne of David his father" will be conceived in the womb of the Virgin of Nazareth by "the power of the Most High." Therefore the words of the prophet Nathan will be fulfilled—literally—because Mary's child is a Son to God and God is Father to her Son. Only in the light of everything we have heard and reflected upon before this final Sunday of Advent can we adequately reflect on the scene St. Luke describes.

The arresting portrait of this young woman who enjoys God's favor and is full of grace is the foundation for everything we believe. Worthily celebrating the birth of her son demands that we take a stance with her and see that our lives, too, are part of the trajectory of divine love that has been the guiding force of human history. Our lives are part of the prophetic fulfillment of which St.

Paul writes, because God's first creative Word was meant to open his life to ours.

Even after we sinned, God continued to be one step ahead us, "wherever [we] went," destroying all of our enemies and preserving us from the afflictions of the wicked. God has never been content to dwell within a tent or even a temple made of human hands. He wants only to dwell within each one of us, where we are and as we are. The child whose birth we are soon to celebrate "will be called holy" because his human flesh is the method by which God dwells permanently with his people.

St. Thérèse understood her place within the trajectory of divine love. She stood with and alongside Mary, Elizabeth, and all other women and men who, in different times, places, and circumstances, knew that nothing is impossible for God. Like them, St. Thérèse freely offered the whole of her life to the plan and often unexpected scope of God's word. She sang "the goodness of the Lord" (Psalm Response, Psalm 89:2) by the way she lived in the quiet confines of the Carmelite cloister. She accepted the overshadowing of the Holy Spirit as she saw that God had chosen to dwell in her flesh and blood. Thus she could spend herself in love as did Mary's Son.

He has no need of our works but only of our love.

Sunday, Week Four, Cycle C
   First Reading: Micah 5:1–4a
   Second Reading: Hebrews 10:5–10
   Gospel: Luke 1:39–45

The Joy of God's Presence

Each one of us may feel at times "too small to be among the clans of Judah." Yet thanks to the fruit of Mary's womb, we have become the body God prepared for his Son. It is through us, as members of his body, the Church, that the peace of the One "whose origin is from of old" reaches "to the ends of the earth."

When Mary had borne her child, human history was changed once and for all. Jesus has consecrated us to God by the offering of his body. In coming to do the Father's will, he made it possible for us to render true and fitting offerings to God—not through "sacrifices and offerings, holocausts and sin offerings," but through the very real situations that shape our lives. What we experience as embodied persons—our desires and drives, our weaknesses, our fatigue—have become suitable means for expressing our love and gratitude to the Father. Learning to be patient and kind, slow to anger and rich in justice, willing to respond to others or simply be present to them—these are means by which we express thankfulness to God. The Lord does not have any interest in "sin offerings"; he does, however, have an active interest in the new life that we receive through the Son.

Each of us should live what Elizabeth knew—namely, that the Mother of God has come to us, bringing her son with her. Our hearts should be as filled with joy as was the child John in the womb of his mother.

How does Jesus come to us? It happens because God, from his "throne upon the cherubim," has "looked down from heaven" and seen our neediness. He sends the Son of Man to shepherd us by giving us "new life," that we may never again withdraw from God or reject his ways (Psalm Response, Psalm 80:2, 15, 19).

Throughout the season of Advent, we have heard over and over again about God's love and care, about his desire to restore and redeem us so that we can return to him and be his forever. Let us listen attentively and prayerfully reflect on what has been proclaimed. Then we, like Mary, must believe that what has been spoken about us will likewise be fulfilled.

St. Thérèse knew that her life was of biblical significance. She read the story of Christ's birth not as an anecdote of the past but as a narrative of her own birth as a child of God. Every town, every human heart, has become a place for the ruler of Israel to be born. There is a hill country to which each one of us must make haste. God longs for each of us to say, in whatever we are asked to do and wherever we are asked to go, "Behold, I come to do your will."

I no longer have any great desires except that of loving to the point of dying of love.

December 17
First Reading: Genesis 49:2, 8–10
Gospel: Matthew 1:1–17

More Than the Family
In these final days before the celebration of Christ's birth, we are "assembled" to "listen to Israel, [our] father." We are expected to listen attentively to the way in which God has chosen, in the words of Psalm 72, to "govern [his] people with justice and [the] afflicted ones with judgment."

The coming of Jesus Christ, "the son of David, the son of Abraham," is the culmination of the course of divine love that reaches as far back as Creation. The moment recorded in today's First Reading is therefore something greater than a father's words about the hopes and the heritage of Judah his son. They are prophetic insofar as they give voice to the arc of God's decisive actions on our behalf.

These moments from our past, preserved and handed down by the Church, are essential for a proper understanding of who God is for us. They reassure us that he has been ever present, straightening the pathways made crooked by distractions and our disinterest in his loving providence.

God guides creation with power and love. So our ears open to the genealogy of Matthew's Gospel as if to the words of a victory song. Every moment it recalls—the election of Abraham, the transformation of a tribe into a nation, the establishment of a king, and even the exile—is a moment in which God has been intimately involved. His sole purpose has been to bless all the peoples of the earth through the kingship of his Son. At no time were we ever alone or unwanted. The family history of Jesus Christ is the history of divine love throughout time. For his justice and peace shall flourish forever.

The genealogy of Jesus is therefore the family history of every Christian. Our union with Christ through baptism draws us into the lives of those Matthew mentions. We must see our lives, in light of today's Gospel passage, as the culmination of God's movement through forty-two generations. Through the humanity of the only begotten Son, we have a share in his divinity.

God has willed from the first moment of creation that we should be one with him forever. By recounting the family history that led to the fulfillment of God's plan, we discover the true nature of salvation: God has been active and attentive throughout each moment of our lives. Christ's return in glory will be the culmination of God's love in action.

I was acting towards Him like a child who believes everything is permitted and looks upon the treasures of its Father as its own.

December 18
  First Reading: Jeremiah 23:5–8
  Gospel: Matthew 1:18–25

Having Our Own Place

As a result of original sin, we were banished from God and alienated from each other. Only the Lord, the God of Israel, could bring us back to him and to one another. His love and care are not memories of the past, such that we recall how once he "brought the children of Israel out of the land of Egypt." Each one of us can say we "live on [our] own land."

"The earth is the LORD's and all that it holds" (Psalm 24:1, *NAB*). Thus we should never be afraid to take his Son or his Son's mother into our homes. Such is the plan for Joseph. God has put into the hands of this "righteous man" the life of his Son, through whom he will free the whole world.

Joseph displays the ultimate disposition of faith by trusting the angel. How easily he could have awakened in doubt and decided to ignore the strange and troubling experience of his sleep. Yet the angel's insistence that Mary's condition fulfills "what the Lord had said through the prophet" made it impossible for this man of faith to discount what had taken place during the night.

Perhaps more than any other biblical figure, Joseph teaches us that authentic trust in God is inextricably linked with trust in the words of Jeremiah and the other prophets. The angel's words are consistent with Joseph's own hope that God will "raise up a righteous shoot to David,…'The Lord our justice.'"

The woman to whom Joseph is betrothed called no attention to herself; in no way would she bring shame or hardship on him. She knew that only God could explain to Joseph the events unfolding in both their lives. How difficult it must have been for Mary to remain quiet and allow the Lord to explain things to Joseph in a way he could grasp. This is how God chose to reveal his mighty power.

The birth of Jesus Christ comes about in such a way that no one is exposed to the law. Even at his birth it is clear that God is with us not to condemn but to give life by saving people from their sins. What is true at the beginning of Jesus's life remains true throughout history, even to his return.

Joseph is like the Son in wanting no one exposed to shame. Jesus wants us all to be overshadowed by the love that describes his life with the Father and the Holy Spirit. At those times when it is difficult to comprehend how our impoverished lives are being saved, we should ask Joseph to take us into his home. There he will reassure us that, truly, "God is with us."

My God, have pity on me; have pity on your little child. Have pity!

December 19

First Reading: Judges 13:2–7, 24–25a

Gospel: Luke 1:5–25

Stirred by the Lord's Spirit

Today we see the salvation story unfold within the parameters of the relationships of two childless couples. In the First Reading, "an angel of God, terrible indeed," appears to an unnamed woman. She is barren, yet the angel says she will conceive and give birth to a son, who "will begin the deliverance of Israel from the power of the Philistines." The woman relates this remarkable experience to her husband, Manoah, and eventually the events come to pass.

In the Gospel it is the husband to whom an angel appears with words that are just as amazing. Although he is a "righteous" man from the "priestly division of Abijah," Zechariah finds the message hard to believe. He is "an old man," and his wife "is advanced in years." The angel quiets Zechariah's fears by literally silencing him.

Astonishment and uncertainty often mark the ways in which Christ comes into our lives. In times of confusion and in periods of doubt, silence can be a welcome companion. It allows us to consider not only the mystery of God made man but also the mystery of man becoming God.

The child Elizabeth will conceive will be "great in the sight of the Lord," because he will go before the Lord "in the spirit and power of Elijah." Not only will Zechariah's son bring joy to his parents, but he will "turn the hearts of fathers toward their children and the disobedient to the understanding of the righteous."

He will "prepare a people fit for the Lord." Zechariah knows that his son will be stirred by the spirit of the Lord.

Every human heart contains a prayer not yet answered and a desire yet to be fulfilled. Like both couples in today's Scriptures, the ways in which God responds to us can be truly unsettling and his purposes difficult to comprehend. Each couple longed for a child, but the lives they conceived were more than just answers to personal prayers. Samson and John both entered the world in order to show the splendor and the glory of God the Father. They were set apart, "taking no wine or drinking strong drink," because they were inebriated by the mighty works and singular justice of God.

In Jesus our disgrace has been removed. God has seen fit to do this in a way far greater than any we could have fashioned for ourselves. Our mouths should sing of God's glory, for he has rescued us from the hand of the wicked and been our strength even from our mother's womb.

Yes, all is well when one seeks only the will of Jesus.

December 20

First Reading: Isaiah 7:10–14

Gospel: Luke 1:26–38

God Provides the Sign

Psalm 24 speaks of a race that "seeks the face of the God of Jacob" (Psalm 24:6). This people could never have imagined the way God would choose to respond to their longing. Imprisoned by sin, they knew better than to tempt the Lord or ask for a sign. So they waited in hope for what today's Alleluia verse describes as the "Key of David." This Key would open for them "the gates of God's eternal Kingdom" and allow them to receive a blessing from the Lord.

The way in which St. Luke records the entrance of the King of Glory shows once again the personal nature of God's saving love. In one sentence we learn the names of the town, the betrothed, and the Virgin. These essential details assert the intention with which God is acting. There is nothing random about God's plan and nothing unforeseen according to his providential care.

We also learn from St. Luke that the young woman "betrothed to a man named Joseph, of the house of David" was not anticipating the visitation of the angel. His greeting would only be troubling to someone who had never considered herself to be privileged or special. She needed the angel to explain the ways of God in order to say yes freely and totally.

In God's eyes we are all special. It can be difficult to accept the fact that God believes in each one of us, especially when we don't believe in ourselves. It can be difficult to recognize just what it is that God sees in us.

Mary helps us understand that the greeting of the angel wasn't meant for her alone. God wants his face to be seen! He wants to be known by every race and tongue, by every people and nation. "Gabriel was sent from God to a town of Galilee called Nazareth" so that the "Son of the Most High" could come to every town, especially the one in which you live.

The celebration of the birth of the Son of God is the celebration of God's allowing us to see him face-to-face. Through the Virgin of Nazareth, we can now look on the face of God and live. We have been freed from the darkness of sin in order to "ascend the mountain of the LORD" and stand with Christ in God's "holy place."

Through the son of the Virgin of Nazareth, we have all found favor, "for nothing will be impossible for God." Through the son of the Virgin of Nazareth, we have received a blessing from the Lord. Thus our hearts should cry out with Mary's, "May it be done to me according to your word."

Ah! what a surprise we shall have at the end of the world when we shall read the story of souls!

December 21

First Reading: Song of Songs 2:8–14

Alternate First Reading: Zephaniah 3:14–18a

Gospel: Luke 1:39–45

Arise and Come!

The prophet Zephaniah reminds us, "The LORD has removed the judgment against" his people. Is there need for anything further?

Sadly, we allow ourselves to become discouraged amid the trying occasions of life. Physical, emotional, financial, and spiritual demands make us doubt the extent to which God is really "in [our] midst." We trade knowledge of our mighty Savior for quick and easy remedies that we believe will renew us in love and restore our lives to what *we* determine they should be.

When Mary set out "in haste" to visit her cousin, joy was her sole motivation. The angel had made it clear that the incomprehensible ways of God are not to be enjoyed alone. God is wonderfully conscious of our human needs, especially in those things that appertain to him. Mary knows that "the LORD has removed the judgment" against humanity and "turned away [all] enemies."

Mary and Elizabeth are perfect mirrors by which the hand of Divine Providence has been revealed. How could the child of Elizabeth's womb not leap for joy in the presence of "the mother of [the] Lord"? How can we not live in joy even now as we—womb-like—await the Lord in the fullness of his glory? The one who is our help and our shield will return to bring us to the place he shares with the Father.

Our hearts should be filled with the same exuberance recorded in the Song of Songs. God loves us! He has always been standing with us, peering into the recesses of our lives, waiting for just the right moment to say, "Arise, my beloved, my dove, my beautiful one, and come!" The winter of sin has passed, and the song of the dove echoes through the land. This is the plan of the Lord that "stands forever" (Psalm Response, Psalm 33:11). The "design of his heart, through all generations" is that we should let him say in the deepest places in our hearts, "You are lovely!"

Elizabeth is rightly "filled with the Holy Spirit," the same Spirit who overshadows the life of everyone who has entered the waters of baptism. We have "no further misfortune to fear." Rather let us believe that everything spoken by the Lord will be fulfilled.

O Jesus, my Divine Spouse! May I never lose the second robe of my baptism!

December 22

First Reading: Samuel 1:24–28

Gospel: Luke 1:46–56

Being Raised Up

Hannah knows well God's promise of mercy. The Lord raised her from the lowliness of infertility and filled her soul with profound joy. Conceiving and bearing the child have been enough to assure Hannah of God's victory in her life. She is willing to share what she wanted most because she knows that the child is not for her alone. She makes a fitting offering to the Lord, giving back to him the child for whom she wept and prayed. Even the boy's father seems to understand: He offers a three-year-old bull, an ephah of flour, and a skin of wine.

Like Hannah before her, Mary knows that her child is not hers alone. The angel announced that God would save people from their sins through the life of the child conceived in her womb by the power of the Holy Spirit. Mary makes her own the words of Hannah, which are used as today's Responsorial Psalm. Mary knows that the fulfillment of all that was said through the prophets happens in the lives of real people, at specific times and according to God's purposes.

Mary's words, as recorded by St. Luke, illustrate perfectly the way in which she has come to understand God, herself, and all of creation. Mary's soul is a lens by which others can see God's love for the human family. Mary's life hasn't added anything to the Lord her savior. On the contrary, God's desire to lift her into his plan of redemption in such an intimately personal way models the dynamic of loving the Lord, heeding his voice, and following his commands.

Like Hannah, Mary will also give back to the Lord what she has received. The act of thanksgiving recorded in the First Reading welcomes the new covenant. God has remembered his promise of mercy. Mary calls all to remember that God has made his glorious throne our heritage.

The song of the young maiden of Nazareth describes the immensity and audacity of God's love. Standing before her cousin and speaking on behalf of Hannah and all great women of her people, Mary gives voice to what every Christian can exclaim: "The Almighty has done great things for me, and holy is his Name."

Oh! everything truly smiled upon me on this earth: I found flowers under each of my steps and my happy disposition contributed much to making life pleasant.

December 23
First Reading: Malachi 3:1–4, 23–24
Gospel: Luke 1:57–66

God Has Prepared Us

In the First Reading the prophet Malachi reminds us that God always prepares the way for us. The act of creation was itself God's first movement toward our lives being united with his. Through the earth, the seas, and all that they contain, God has made known to us his ways and shown us his paths (see Psalm Response, Psalm 25:4). We have only to "lift up [our] heads and see" that our "redemption is near at hand" (Psalm Response; see Luke 21:28).

This is the consistent message of Sacred Scripture. This is the Good News we are about to celebrate in Christ's birth.

Elizabeth is certainly ready to celebrate the way in which God has shown great mercy toward her. With scandalous insistence she declares that her child "will be called John," a name completely disconnected from her and Zechariah's ancestors. Elizabeth knows that God is establishing a new genealogy, one that doesn't eradicate the old but raises it to greater heights. Elizabeth knows that the generation of real life can only come from God and not through the normal course of procreation.

Something new is about to begin, and Elizabeth is preparing the way for it. Even Zechariah's imposed silence is lifted so that he can bear witness to what Elizabeth has grasped through the events unfolding in her life and that of her cousin Mary.

Time and again we need to grasp Christ's coming as it unfolds in our lives. We celebrate not anecdotes from the past but events from the present and moments of our future. God has chosen to establish his dwelling among us through the flesh of the Virgin

Mary. Unworthy as we may be, the Lord did not see fit to hold our disgrace against us. God has chosen to show us the way in kindness and in friendship. Though formed from the dust, we have been given the breath of eternal life. Oh, that our hearts might turn once more to the heart of our eternal Father!

On the day that John is marked with the sign of the old covenant, circumcision, Elizabeth's words make it clear that her son will prepare people for a new covenant. The fear that falls upon those gathered prepares them for the matters that are being discussed to this day. The people of the hill country of Judea know that the hand of the Lord is upon the child John, even as they wonder what he might be.

We know John; we know who he is and why he came. We should therefore accept what Elizabeth knew: "Good and upright is the LORD" (Psalm Response, Psalm 25:8), for his heart is forever turned toward his children.

I can no longer ask for anything with fervor except the accomplishment of God's will in my soul without any creature being able to set obstacles in the way.

Mass in the Morning on December 24
    First Reading: 2 Samuel 7:1–5, 8b–12, 14a, 16
    Gospel: Luke 1:67–79

Rest From Our Enemies

It is easy to become "settled" in our spiritual lives. The seasons of the liturgical year are meant to arouse us to reflect upon our lives and meditate upon the ways of God. This is exactly what David does in today's First Reading.

David is settled in his palace. He has rest from all his enemies, and this affords him a chance to consider his relationship with God. The fruit of this reflection is the desire to build a fitting house for the ark of God, which has been in a tent.

The prophet Nathan welcomes this and sets David on course— until God says otherwise. It isn't that Nathan is unfamiliar with the ways of God; it is simply that God's ways are not ours. David's intentions are good and honorable, but God has something better in mind. That's what we will be celebrating tomorrow.

Zechariah learned through silence what David and Nathan were to learn from the Lord. The manner by which God has chosen to come to his people and set them free, the way in which he has chosen to dwell among his people, is far beyond any "house" men might build for God. The oath sworn to Abraham is about to be fulfilled through the forgiveness of sins. A new era is about to dawn on the human family, one in which the "tender compassion of our God" will pierce the darkness of sin and death and lead us into the peace that only God can give.

We can all cry out to God, "You are my Father," because of the birth that is celebrated tomorrow! Now and forever the splendor of eternal light shines upon the human family through the flesh of the Virgin's Son. Tomorrow we celebrate the fulfillment of every word, gesture, and action of the prophets. We celebrate the path to solace and relief. We celebrate God's coming to us at the very time his kindness could be established forever.

Zechariah, "filled with the Holy Spirit," sings the opening hymn of the new covenant. In Christ our offerings become the Lord's own offerings, and we are made pure, cleansed of our sins and alive with new vigor. Zechariah's child will indeed be called "the prophet of the Most High," because he will go before the Lord, preparing Christ's way. John will prepare people for the mighty Savior raised up from the flesh of the Virgin Mary.

The child born of the house of David has come to save us from our enemies and free us from the hands of all who hate us. Oh, come, let us adore him!

I wanted to amuse little Jesus, to give Him pleasure; I wanted to give myself up to His childish whims. He heard my prayer.

The Christmas Season

It was December 25, 1886, that I received the grace of leaving my childhood, in a word, the grace of my complete conversion....

On that night of light began the third period of my life, the most beautiful and the most filled with graces from heaven. The work I had been unable to do in ten years was done by Jesus in one instant, contenting himself with my good will which was never lacking.

Vigil Mass for Christmas
First Reading: Isaiah 62:1–5
Second Reading: Acts of the Apostles 13:16–17, 22–25
Gospel: Matthew 1:1–25

God Is With Us!

"When Joseph awoke" he did exactly what each one of us must do: take Christ into our homes. The fear Joseph initially felt gives way to trust, because "the angel of the Lord" reminds him of his place within the genealogy recounted at the beginning of Matthew's Gospel. Joseph, "son of David," should be fearless because the child has been conceived through the power of the Holy Spirit.

These words of the angel correspond to the ancient hope Joseph shares with his people. Israel looks forward to the time when God will lead them from their "desolate" and "forsaken" condition and once again take delight in them. He will rejoice with the Israelites "as a bridegroom rejoices in his bride."

The Second Reading and the Gospel both take us back to the moment when God extended the hand of friendship to Abraham and his descendants. The path of history recounted in this evening's readings remind us that the coming of Christ is part of a plan formed long ago, a plan that will ultimately reunite us with the God who has always been on our side. Although it may seem like a dream that "God is with us," this is in truth why Jesus has come. It is the reason he can save us from our sins.

Thus God extends a hand of friendship to Joseph, a man whose righteousness is perfectly expressed by his obedience to the words of the angel. If Mary's Son has indeed been conceived by the power of the Holy Spirit, then God has chosen the most unimagined way to speak his creative Word into human history. What is surely a dream can be accepted by a man whose faith is rooted in God's promise to establish the throne of David for all generations.

God has chosen Joseph for a special place in his plan of redemption because Joseph, like David before him, is a man after the Lord's own heart. His willingness to take Mary into his home forever transforms him into an image of the Father. The "Builder" longs to marry his people "as a young man marries a virgin."

This evening the Scriptures invite us to be like the man Joseph. We are asked to betroth ourselves to God by taking his Son into our hearts. Through Christ we can trace our lineage back to Abraham; we have a rightful place within the trajectory of salvation history.

St. Thérèse knew that the celebration of Christmas is more than just a mystery of God becoming man. She knew it as the celebration of God and man becoming espoused. The birth of Christ is the decisive expression of God rejoicing in his children. Although we are not worthy to unfasten the sandals on Christ's feet, he will loosen the chains that bind our hearts, freeing them to sing forever the goodness of the Lord.

On that night when He made Himself subject to weakness and suffering for love of me, He made me strong and courageous, arming me with His weapons.

Christmas Mass at Midnight
  First Reading: Isaiah 9:1–6
  Second Reading: Titus 2:11–14
  Gospel: Luke 2:1–14

The Zeal of the Lord

Tonight we are reminded that the grace of God appeared in the most unthinkable way. A multitude of the heavenly host announces to a band of shepherds that they will find the Savior of the world "in swaddling clothes and lying in a manger." In the city of David lies the infant who has come to smash "the yoke that burdened them, the pole on their shoulder, and the rod of their taskmaster."

Perhaps the sign they are given reminds them of the words of the prophet Isaiah. Thus they set out in haste to see this "Wonder-Counselor, God-Hero, Father-Forever, Prince of Peace." In an ordinary human place, they encounter what St. Paul describes as "the appearance of the glory of our great God."

The light that shatters the darkness of those living "in a land of gloom" emanates from within the confines of an official decree, Joseph's family history, displaced lodgings, and a borrowed manger. The good news proclaimed by the angels is a light that blinds all human notions of grandeur and power. The "zeal of the Lord of Hosts" will not be revealed through force or violence, nor by manipulation and control, but in the simple dignity of a mother giving birth "to her firstborn son." The peace of which the angels sing will dawn within the hearts of those who accept God's favor. The glory of God is revealed through our humanity, as the shepherds encounter it in the infant.

By his birth our "savior Jesus Christ" gives himself up for us, "to deliver us from all lawlessness and to cleanse" us of our sins. The humble nature of his birth foretells the whole of his life as man. The "Prince of Peace" is born as one like us so that we can be born into the righteousness of God (see 2 Corinthians 5:21). Already his birth counsels us that the ways of God are far above the ways of men.

As Christ comes into the world, so God peers into the very depths of our condition. He knows the worldly desires that prevent us from seeing ourselves as we truly are. If like the shepherds we can accept the testimony of the angel and kneel before the child lying in the manger, then God can fulfill the deepest desires of our hearts. He can make us "eager to do what is good" if we but ask.

Just as God's love came into the world in the humble, ordinary way celebrated tonight, so can his love be revealed through our own lives. St. Thérèse teaches us how the most ordinary moments can manifest the extraordinary and unexpected "zeal of the LORD of Hosts." The glory of the Lord is revealed through love.

I felt charity enter into my soul, and the need to forget myself and to please others; since then I've been happy!

Christmas Mass at Dawn

First Reading: Isaiah 62:11–12

Second Reading: Titus 3:4–7

Gospel: Luke 2:15–20

God's Kind and Generous Love

At dawn we learn of our Savior through the lens of the shepherds and the heart of Mary. For the shepherds the presence of the angels is just as significant as their message. What God makes known corresponds to the desire of every human heart: to know beyond all doubt that God has not forsaken us, that he loves and cares for us.

The shepherds make haste to "see this thing that has taken place, which the Lord has made known." They do not doubt what they have heard and seen, but they want to participate in God's saving mercy. When they find "Mary and Joseph, and the infant lying in the manger," they become God's messengers. Like the angels, they glorify and praise God for all that they have seen and heard. The light that appeared in the sky is now a light that shines from their lives, such that all who hear them will be amazed.

Once the light of God's love dawns within our hearts, we too must be heralds of the good news the angels announced and custodians of the events the shepherds made known. The gift of Christ's mercy is meant for the whole world. Jesus is born into the world to offer the saving "bath of rebirth and renewal by the Holy Spirit" to everyone, everywhere, in every time.

Through the birth of the child, grace is poured into the world. Like the shepherds, those who have received this grace must let all people see God's glory in every circumstance of their lives.

We learn from Mary just what it means to be a custodian of the event we celebrate this morning. Like her we must take to heart the way in which God has chosen to appear, especially as it owes nothing to "any righteous deeds we [have] done." Taking to heart the events recounted in this morning's Gospel opens the whole of our lives to the grace that justifies us and secures us in the "hope of eternal life."

Like Mary's, our lives must be expressions of an ongoing and ever-deepening reflection on the amazing things the shepherds tell. Securing our hearts this way ensures that the hope born into the world will spill into our lives. It also ensures that our lives will even now spill over into everlasting life.

This vibrant reciprocity between our present and our eternal destinies led St. Thérèse of Lisieux to declare that heaven is now! She knew that, through her baptism into Christ, she already shared in the life the shepherds made haste to see. She knew that the light that shone on Christmas morning has never been extinguished! It is a light that every Christian must carry and keep brightly shining until Christ returns in glory. This light is a gift of peace and a sign of God's unending favor.

When the human heart gives itself to God, it loses nothing of its innate tenderness; in fact, this tenderness grows when it becomes more pure and more divine.

Christmas Mass During the Day
   First Reading: Isaiah 52:7–10
   Second Reading: Hebrews 1:1–6
   Gospel: John 1:1–18

"In the Beginning"
The Word by whom God "created the universe" enters the world just as we have. This Word brings glad tidings and announces peace and salvation. This Word "became flesh" in order to make his dwelling among us, so that all men might receive "grace in place of grace."

There is nothing "partial" about the way in which the glory of the Father's only begotten Son has been revealed. In the birth of Jesus, God has "bared his holy arm:" It is the arm of a vulnerable child. The Word by which the world came to be does not overwhelm us with its creative power or unconquerable strength. Rather, this Word to which John testified has come to us in the utter simplicity of a child.

The feet that bring such glad tidings are actually not "beautiful"; they are scorched and calloused from running through hot sands, over rocks and stones, and through desert places to announce salvation and say, "Your God is King!" Their beauty is found in the joy that lets them suffer gladly as testimony to the light that gives us the "power to become children of God." It is a beauty that will be revealed when the feet of the man Jesus are nailed to the cross.

The true light that has come into the world this Christmas Day is "the light of the human race," for it alone brings lasting comfort. "In the sight of all the nations," God has come to ask for our love. By the humble nature of his birth, Jesus, the "Word that was from the beginning," speaks to us about the littleness of God as the essence of true love. For on this day God has given himself to us in the gift of his Son, asking only that we welcome him, care for him, and learn from him. On this day God asks us to believe in the name that is "the imprint of his being," in order that we might see in the face of Jesus the God whom we cannot see.

The Word that was with God in the beginning speaks to the dignity of human nature, and by his birth today he more wondrously restores that dignity. His truth continues to radiate through the lives of St. Thérèse of Lisieux and all the saints. They rightly believed that the dignity of being human was fully manifested through love. All in their own days emptied themselves and took up the way of renunciation as their way of sharing the love of a Father's only Son. Within their impoverished and fragile flesh, the saints learned the secret of that Word that was with the Father "in the beginning." By their own neediness they gave back to God the gift he first gave us, when "the Word became flesh and made his dwelling among us."

Jesus deigned to show me the road that leads to this Divine Furnace, and this road is the surrender of the little child who sleeps without fear in its Father's arms.

December 26

The Feast of St. Stephen

First Reading: Acts of the Apostles 6:8–10; 7:54–59

Gospel: Matthew 10:17–22

Looking to Christ

The coming of God as man is an invitation for each one of us to do as Stephen did: to commend our spirits to the Lord. This is necessary if we are to "endure to the end." Stephen's death shows us that we can in fact be witnesses for Jesus—in courts, before governors and kings, before all who do not believe.

In today's Gospel Jesus is quite clear about the cost of discipleship. He wants no one to follow him blindly. The only safeguard we have, even against members of our own families, is to be filled with the Holy Spirit. When the Spirit is in communion with our own spirits, we will be able to welcome the wisdom with which he inspires us to speak and act. The only thing the world can do against the wisdom of the Holy Spirit is to mock what we say— or hand us over to death.

By his birth Jesus reveals the extent to which God is in solidarity with us. By his death Stephen reveals the extent to which we are called to be in solidarity with God. *Communion with God* not only expresses how divine life flows into our lives here and now but also describes how the circumstances of our lives flow into the life of the divine.

That is why Stephen can "look intently to heaven" and see "the glory of God and Jesus standing at the right hand of God." The meeting of God with man in Christ draws our lives into every facet of the life of Christ. His experiences and his words mingle with our own. We should be able to say with St. Paul, at whose feet the witnesses against Stephen here lay down their cloaks, "I live, no longer I, but Christ lives in me" (Galatians 2:20, *NAB*).

The revelation of the Father's love in the birth of Jesus is inseparable from the revelation of the Father's love in the death of his Son. The love drawing us to the manger will draw us likewise to the cross. The vulnerability of the child will be displayed again when Jesus is condemned by a court and handed over to death. The Father's love endures to the end, when Jesus commends his spirit to the Father. Love is the salvation of man. It is a love that hopes all things, suffers all things, and like Stephen, forgives all things (see 1 Corinthians 13:5–7).

Jesus knew how to pray for his persecutors because he knew how to pray for us. Stephen could forgive those infuriated by his words because he saw himself as one who, because of sin, had "persecuted" God.

The scene recounted in the Acts of the Apostles will leave an indelible mark on the young Saul. It should leave an indelible mark on each of us. Like Stephen, we should willingly commend our spirits to Jesus and be filled with grace and power. Then we too will work "great signs and wonders among the people" that desperately need to know the love of God in Christ Jesus his Son.

I will teach you how to travel…with the surrender and the love of a child who knows his Father loves him and cannot leave him alone in the hour of danger.

December 27

The Feast of St. John the Evangelist

First Reading: 1 John 1:1–4

Gospel: John 20:1a, 2–8

Christmas Is Not a Memory

When St. John goes into the tomb, he sees and believes what he has hoped from the beginning—namely, that our lives mean something to God, that his commitment to us is not just an idea or a noble sentiment. God's belief in us can be seen and heard and touched.

What was from the beginning is the presence of God now made visible in the flesh and blood of Jesus Christ. John can peer into the empty tomb and believe this as the most reasonable explanation for what he sees. The resurrection of Jesus from the dead is the only fitting conclusion to the Word becoming flesh to dwell among us.

The resurrection of Christ guarantees that the story of Christmas does not remain in the past. What we celebrate is not an anecdote from history but the truth of our own existence. In having "fellowship…with the Father and with his Son," we become the flesh and blood by which the story continues to be heard and seen, touched and felt, in every time and place, in all situations and circumstances. The Lord has not been taken from us. By his resurrection from the dead, Jesus is able to give himself to us, that where he is we might also be.

The fellowship we share with one another in the Lord ensures that "the first day of the week" never ends! The joy that John feels among the company of friends who share his life in Christ is the same joy for which Christ prayed on the night before he died (see

John 15:11). Through the apostle we can see the signs pointing us to our destiny in Christ. God continues to make himself seen and heard and touched, to paraphrase Pope Benedict XVI, person, by person, by person.

The one we kneel to gaze upon in the manger is the one who kneels before us to wash our feet and cleanse us of our sins. He is the one who, under the appearance of bread and wine, humbles himself to nourish and sustain our life in him. The one lying helpless in the manger is the one who will hang helpless on the cross. All this is so that the Father can reach out to us in love.

The apostles Peter and John "both ran" to the tomb of Jesus. They were running toward the hope awakened in them on the day they abandoned their nets and followed Jesus. If the tomb was empty, then the Word that was from the beginning had not been silenced!

Indeed, the horror of the cross was not the end of the Christmas story; it was merely its explanation. By his words recorded in Scripture, John continues to give thanks to God's holy name, so that all may have fellowship with Christ.

This was really his day of triumph.

December 28

The Feast of the Holy Innocents
First Reading: 1 John 1:5—2:2
Gospel: Matthew 2:13–18

Mistaken for Christ

While there is "no darkness at all" in God, today's Gospel vividly recounts the darkness that can be found within the human heart. The horror of Herod's massacre should remind us of the need "to walk in the light" and allow the blood of Jesus to cleanse us of all sin. For as John proclaims, in Jesus Christ "we have an Advocate with the Father," so we should never be afraid to acknowledge our sins. This constant recourse to Christ allows the faith we profess to shape the manner in which we live.

Amid the "sobbing and loud lamentation" over the deaths of the Holy Innocents, the light of God continues to shine. The unspoken witness the young martyrs bear in being mistaken for Christ should instill in our hearts a desire to become like little children. Jesus, by becoming one like us, made it impossible for Herod to determine his identity. The light that dawns from the martyrdom of these boys should console all those who mourn their passing.

The appearance of God does not instantly change the world: Darkness is not immediately overcome. But human hearts are changed. Already we have celebrated the changes in Mary's troubled heart (see Luke 1:29) and in Joseph's (see Matthew 2:20). Surely the magi have followed the star in the hope of a new worldview.

Christmas is the celebration of a presence that touches our hearts. Like the magi, we return from the crib "by another way"

(Matthew 2:12, *NAB*), for we have seen God, ourselves, others, and all of creation in a whole new light. This light that illumines our new way is truth and life. It frees us from all the snares of the evil one and draws us into fellowship with God and our neighbor.

All martyrs have walked in the light of this new way. The innocent boys whose lives were shattered by the darkness of Herod's heart live perpetually in this light. Their witness confirms what today's psalm proclaims,

> Our help is in the name of the LORD,
>   who made heaven and earth." (Psalm 124:8)

It seems to me that the darkness, borrowing the voice of sinners, says mockingly to me: "You are dreaming about the light."

December 29

Fifth Day in the Octave of Christmas

First Reading: 1 John 2:3–11

Gospel: Luke 2:22–35

Walking With Christ

Once again we learn that God has come into the world to open the ordinary moments of life to the unexpected and extraordinary. The parents of Jesus take him to Jerusalem, because it is "written in the law of the Lord, *Every male shall be consecrated to the Lord*." Because Mary and Joseph do what is required, God is able to reveal the "salvation [he] prepared, a light for revelation to the Gentiles, and glory for…Israel."

Simeon, a man righteous and devout, has been "awaiting the consolation of Israel," with a promise from God that he will not see death before laying eyes on Christ. Moved by the Spirit to come to the temple, he encounters the child "destined for the fall and rise of many." In the ordinary rites commanded by the law, Simeon has the extraordinary privilege of not only seeing but also holding within his aged, hope-filled hands the glory of Israel. For years Simeon has been true to God's commandments; today "the love of God is truly perfected in him."

The parents of Jesus are amazed at Simeon's words and at everything that takes place in the temple. Their disposition shows us that the plan of God to which they have both given their lives is not static. Its dynamic nature is perfectly demonstrated by Mary and Joseph's willingness to "walk just as" their Son will walk, even though it means that a sword shall pierce the mother's heart.

Mary and Joseph "keep God's commandments," and this now becomes the way that will lead to greater knowledge of their Son.

He is the "true light" that is already pushing aside the darkness in the world. Mary and Joseph will see this light shine ever more brightly. Thus many will come to believe in their son, and these "will not perish, but…have eternal life" (John 3:16, *NAB*).

We are not in darkness! Like Simeon, we celebrate the fact that we have seen the fulfillment of God's word and the salvation he has prepared for us in the child born Christmas Day.

The light of Christ has been entrusted to each of us through the waters of rebirth. The power of the Holy Spirit overshadows our lives with the extraordinary grandeur of the temple not made by human hands.

We, too, must be willing to walk the way of Jesus, all the way to the cross. On the hill of Calvary, God's glory will be fully revealed and his words wonderfully fulfilled. On that hill the Christ will disperse the darkness by his unyielding love for all women and men. There we draw the strength "to love our brother" and keep the light of Mary and Joseph's son burning brightly.

I understand now that charity consists in bearing with the faults of others, in not being surprised at their weakness, in being edified by the smallest acts of virtue we see them practice.

December 30
Sixth Day in the Octave of Christmas
First Reading: 1 John 2:12–17
Gospel: Luke 2:36–40

Christ Changes the World

In today's liturgy we are asked to remain just a bit longer in the temple with Mary, Joseph, and the child Jesus. The purpose of our stay is to meet the prophetess Anna. This "daughter of Phanuel" has spent her life worshiping God day and night, "with fasting and prayer." She represents more than the expectant longing of her people: Anna represents what it means to have faith in God, to believe that God will fulfill his promises.

Anna does not "love the world or the things of this world." She chooses instead to love the things of God. Perhaps because she is a widow, she knows well that "all that is in the world" is passing away. The only way to live is to do the will of the Father.

In Mary and Joseph, Anna encounters kindred spirits, and perhaps this is what arouses in her heart the recognition that the redemption of Israel is at hand. Although she knows nothing of the details concerning God's plan, her life of prayer enables her to see in the child Jesus something she has never seen before. She recognizes that a great light has come upon the earth. This changes Anna's world: She now speaks "about the child to all…awaiting the redemption of Jerusalem."

Mary and Joseph fulfill the prescriptions of the law, despite all that they are hearing about their child. God continues to educate them about his Son, and Mary and Joseph humbly submit to this instruction. They return to their home in Nazareth, where they remain a father getting to know "him who is from the beginning" and a mother who has literally carried the love of the Father within her. Jesus will grow strong and be filled with wisdom. He will experience the favor of God through the parents who have been entrusted with his care.

We remain a bit longer in the temple because we, too, have been entrusted with the care of Christ. We, too, can "give thanks to God" and speak about Christ to all those we meet in the way the Spirit inspires. Unlike Anna, we don't have to spend our days in the temple, because our bodies have become temples of the Holy Spirit. God is always with us. Through prayer, fasting, and acts of charity, we can resist "sensual lust, enticement for the eyes, and a pretentious life" and instead do "the will of God."

Then we can sincerely follow the command of today's Responsorial Psalm, "Say among the nations: The LORD is king" (Psalm 96:10).

Christ's birth into our lives is only the beginning. Through faith we recognize the signs of God's glory and the guarantee of the fulfillment of his promises for us. Through faith we awaken each day to a new beginning such as Anna experienced. It is the glory that made the angels sing, brought the shepherds to Bethlehem, and granted the favor of God to humble parents. Through faith we fulfill the prescriptions of the law Christ has given us.

God would have to work a little miracle to make me grow up in an instant, and this miracle He performed on that unforgettable Christmas day.

December 31

Seventh Day in the Octave of Christmas

First Reading: 1 John 2:18–21

Gospel: John 1:1–18

The Truth of Our Being

St. John can tell us that "it is the last hour" because "with the Lord one day is like a thousand years and a thousand years like one day" (2 Peter 3:8, *NAB*). Every day is a chance for us to be once again immersed in the Word that was with God "in the beginning." Every day is an opportunity to be renewed by God's original desire that we share his life and live in his love.

Creation was not an accident of elemental forces randomly combining. In the beginning God intended to create out of nothing, and he imbued that which he spoke into existence with meaning and purpose. "The anointing" we have received "from the Holy One" confirms this truth about each and every one of us: We matter to God! This truth gives us the "power to become children of God," born "not by natural generation nor by human choice nor by a man's decision but of God." The Word that was "with God" in the beginning became flesh to secure this truth. He shows us through his life as a man that what God intended from the beginning is still his plan.

This last day of the calendar year, the Gospel draws our attention to the beginning—to our origins and to the life that is "the light of the human race." We celebrate the fact that the Word fills our lives with grace and truth and has become for us the human face of God. Today the Scriptures remind us that the Word that was with God in the beginning makes the whole of our lives radiant.

The celebration of Christmas is likewise a celebration of creation and the constancy with which God looks with favor on his people. Therefore each day should be for us a renewed experience of having been willed into existence by God, a renewed experience of time, of life, and of salvation. The birth of Christ established the beginning and the fulfillment of all religion. By our share in his life, we can live the last hour as if it were the first. We can say, "day after day," that the Lord rules the earth and the world with justice.

"In the beginning, when God created the heavens and the earth" (Genesis 1:1, *NAB*), he already saw the fulfillment of his plan. He even now sees our fulfillment. We testify to this truth when we allow the Light to shine through us. The darkness cannot overcome this Light.

Let us hold firm to the anointing we have received, for we are the people full of grace and truth whom Christ has gathered to himself.

No, there is no one who could frighten me, for I know too well what to believe concerning His Mercy and His Love.

Feast of the Holy Family, Cycle A
  First Reading: Sirach 3:2–7, 12–14
  Second Reading: Colossians 3:12–21
  Gospel: Matthew 2:13–15, 19–23

Life in the Family

The family life of Jesus took shape according to the words of Sacred Scripture. "When the magi had departed," Joseph is told in a dream of Herod's ferocious anger and horrific plan. Thus the child and his parents flee to Egypt, "that what the Lord had said through the prophet might be fulfilled."

The family remains there until Joseph learns in another dream that Herod has died. Rather than risk settling in Judea, where Herod's son Archelaus now reigns, Joseph takes the child and his mother to the region of Galilee. There they settle in the town of Nazareth, once again fulfilling what was spoken through a prophet, "He shall be called a Nazorean."

The life of every Christian family should likewise be shaped and guided by Sacred Scripture. God no longer has to speak to us through dreams: The Church has preserved, passed down, and interpreted his living Word. Patterning life in the family according to the respect and honor described in today's First Reading transforms the home into a school of communion, where we learn what it means to be human.

Christ calls us to enjoy his own peace. The extent to which we realize this peace depends upon our readiness to bear with one another in love and to forgive whatever grievances we have against another, "as the Lord has forgiven us." We learn to "put on heartfelt compassion, kindness, humility, gentleness and patience."

The home that Mary and Joseph established in Nazareth bears the privilege that every Christian home should have. Holiness of life is a grace for all families who have faith in God and live in obedience to his will. The simple lesson families can learn from Nazareth is to do "everything in the name of the Lord Jesus."

We should strive each day to walk in God's ways. And we know that his commandments are not burdensome, for they correspond perfectly to our desire to love. Mutual and reciprocal self-giving allows the Word of Christ to dwell in the home and secures each member in "the bond of perfection."

Nazareth helps us see our families within the prism of God's saving love and the trajectory of his plan of redemption. We learn to appreciate the lives that make up our home. We see what it means to subordinate ourselves in love. We share in the love that led Jesus to take up his cross and die on Calvary.

Ah! how deep was my emotion when I found myself under the same roof as the Holy Family, contemplating the walls upon which Jesus cast His sacred glance, treading the ground bedewed with the sweat of St. Joseph, under this roof where Mary had carried Jesus in her arms.

Feast of the Holy Family, Cycle B
First Reading: Genesis 15:1–6; 21:1–3
Second Reading: Hebrews 11:8, 11–12, 17–19
Gospel: Luke 2:22–40

God Is Trustworthy

Today's readings place before us one family from the old covenant and one from the new. Each family teaches us that faith is openness to the incomprehensible ways of God.

Abram learns this fundamental characteristic of faith when, against everything he knows, he yields to God's promise to make his descendants as numerous as the stars in the sky. Abram has already determined to experience the "gifts" God has promised by making one of his servants his heir. Then God takes him outside and reminds him of who is the Creator of family life: Only God can guarantee that Abram's "own issue shall be [his] heir."

When Sarah becomes pregnant, Abram realizes that God has taken hold of their destiny, and so he puts his faith in God. The supernatural gift to the couple is the child to whom Abram gives the name Isaac.

The Second Reading recalls God's apparent shattering of Abraham's family life: his asking Abraham to offer Isaac. The faith that gave Abraham and Sarah the power to generate human life is being tested. Abraham is able to submit to God's request because he has already seen God bring life from a man advanced in years and a sterile woman. So surely God is "able to raise even from the dead."

The new covenant family also presents the fundamental characteristic of faith as openness to the incomprehensibility of God.

Although Joseph is not physically the father of Jesus, he has given himself entirely to the generative power of God by which his betrothed is with child. The boy he takes to the temple is, like Isaac, a miraculous gift from God. Joseph presents two turtle doves as the fitting way for a poor man to offer back the gift he has received. By fulfilling all that is required of him, Joseph learns that his child "is destined for the fall and rise of many."

Through the angel Gabriel God has shared with Mary the unsettling scope of his plan, just as angels told Sarah of God's plan for her family. Now Mary learns from Simeon that her miraculous gift from God is for "many hearts," and that her own will be pierced. Once more the test of her faith lies in her willingness to say yes to God.

The lives of these two families, and the lives of all families, have their origins in God. The strength of a family depends upon each individual's willingness to accept from God both the incomprehensible and the heartrending. The strength of every family is built upon the same trusting faith depicted today in the lives of Abraham and Sarah and Joseph and Mary.

Everyone will see that everything comes from God.

Feast of the Holy Family, Cycle C
  First Reading: 1 Samuel 1:20–22, 24–28
  Second Reading: 1 John 3:1–2, 21–24
  Gospel: Luke 2:41–52

The House of the Lord

Hannah and Mary, each in a different way, teach us about the meaning of being "God's children now." Hannah teaches us that every child belongs to God, even the son for whom she desperately prayed. God alone is Father to us all, so no one has a claim on another. Because we are "God's children now," our relationship with him should define and determine all other relationships, even within the family.

Hannah also teaches us that, for the Father's love to be the foundation of our lives, we must have an intense spiritual life. This alone makes us attentive to the voice of God speaking within the depths of our hearts. Surely her unceasing prayer for a child has opened her to God's Spirit in a deeper way. Thus she recognizes the importance of raising her son for God. She freely offers back the beautiful gift God has given her.

Hannah is not concerned with what "has not yet been revealed." What has come to light in her life is the fact that God walks with her and Elkanah. She leaves Samuel at the temple in Shiloh, knowing the happiness that will come to him from dwelling in the house of the Lord.

Mary teaches us that God has come to dwell in our homes in a fully human way. Although Jesus "must be in [his] Father's house," Mary's rightful concern for her Son becomes the means by which the house of the Lord is now widened to include every home. For every family is established to be the dwelling place of God.

By asking her Son why he has done what he has, Mary demonstrates the passion with which she has accepted her responsibility to raise the Son of God. She is to prepare him for what will later be. She knows that her child is holy, but she also knows that the One who gave him has built her family to be the one in which Jesus will grow to manhood.

By going "down with them…to Nazareth," Jesus underscores the lessons we learn from Hannah and Mary. He will advance in wisdom, age, and favor in the home God has made for him with Mary and Joseph. Jesus will be obedient to Mary and Joseph because this is the proper way of children. Through this obedience Jesus will in fact be busy with his Father's affairs.

Hannah and Mary teach us that there is no difficult situation that we cannot adequately confront when "we keep his commandments and do what pleases him." They teach us how to build our faith, so that the strength of God's Spirit lives in us and we can love one another. These are the Father's affairs about which we should be busy.

What He does reserve for us is His Palace of glory where we shall see Him…in the brightness of His infinite splendor!"

January 1

The Solemnity of Mary, Mother of God

First Reading: Numbers 6:22–27

Second Reading: Galatians 4:4–7

Gospel: Luke 2:16–21

Vocation Is Fulfillment

Today in Mary, the Mother of God, we see the embodiment of the prayer of blessing recorded in the First Reading. We learn from her life what it means to have the Lord "bless…and let his face shine" upon us. We see how he looks kindly upon us and gives us peace. Through the record of Sacred Scripture, Mary's way has been made "known upon earth," in order that we may understand the adoption we have received as sons and daughters of God (Psalm Response, Psalm 67:3).

The way of Mary is what the Church refers to as a vocation. Each of us is asked to serve the Father's plan in a unique way. We are not interchangeable, nor are we unessential. God makes himself vulnerable before each one of us, as he did before Mary, inviting us to serve his plan of redemption in the way chosen for us from all eternity.

Mary challenges us to consider human fulfillment within the light of what the Father asks us to do. She teaches us that vocation expands our lives; it doesn't limit them. The vocation to which God invites us requires that we, like Mary, unite our freedom with the freedom of God.

Although the shepherds don't know it at the time, going in haste to Bethlehem moves them toward their vocation. When they find "Mary and Joseph, and the infant lying in the manger," they recognize an invitation to tell everyone "the message that had been told them about this child." This is their vocation.

The Mother of God continues to teach us that loving and serving the Lord through one's vocation is not at odds with being human. Embracing God's call offers us the chance right now to experience the fact that we are not slaves but children of the Father. Our vocations, if freely accepted, push aside all personal fears and challenge us to risk the wonder and splendor of living openly and only for God.

Mary's motherhood, given to us at the foot of the cross (see John 19:27), allows us to draw from the rich treasury of the things she kept in her heart. She encourages us to become custodians of memory, champions of all that is essential, heralds of the truth. Her physical body and her spiritual life confirm the fact that with God all things are possible.

Father encouraged me to be devout to the Blessed Virgin and I promised myself to redouble my tenderness for her.

January 2
First Reading: 1 John 2:22–28
Gospel: John 1:19–28

It's Not About World Peace

Jesus the Christ, Incarnate of the Virgin Mary, was born into the world for something far greater than world peace, sustainable political structures, or a new social order. God's only begotten Son came into the world as man to give us "eternal life." This is what was heard "from the beginning." This is the message of the voice "crying out in the desert." The "anointing that [we] received" secures us in this truth, the only possibility for the transformation of the world.

The world as we know it is passing away, just as it was for the men and women who crossed the Jordan to be baptized by John. He purified them in the waters of the Jordan in preparation for the unimaginable gift that only the Father's Son could give. This gift would unite their lives with his and be the foundation for the hope that characterizes our proper stance before the world. This hope prevents the arduous experiences of life from crushing our spirits or determining our behavior. We remain in this hope to the extent that we accept the purpose of Christ's coming.

Confusion over the reason for Christ's coming is as prevalent today as it was when John baptized. The people who question John have a narrow view of the Christ and what he comes to accomplish. But John knows that Jesus is mightier than any religious or political leader, any movement, any theory or way of life. John knows that Jesus comes to us with the power of an unyielding, unending, and indestructible love—the love of the

Father. The love Jesus offers compels John to describe him as one "whose sandal strap I am not worthy to untie."

The "saving power of God" is perfectly revealed through love (Responsorial Psalm, Psalm 98:3). The Lord makes his salvation known when his Son willingly lays down his life on the cross. The truth we have heard from "the beginning" has everything to do with the cross. So, too, the birth of Jesus. The child we behold in the manger is the same fragile man we behold on Good Friday. Love makes us vulnerable, so we shouldn't be surprised that God's love is likewise revealed in vulnerability.

The priests and Levites who question John were hoping he was the Christ. They hoped to control and manipulate his behavior. Little did they realize that John knew full well who he was and what he was about "across the Jordan." Nor can they imagine that God will express his love by having his Son subordinate himself to their disordered purposes.

Jesus did not come to establish peace on the earth. He came to unite heaven and earth and bring us everlasting life.

Yes, in order that Love be fully satisfied, it is necessary that It lower Itself, and that It lower Itself into nothingness and transform this nothingness into fire.

January 3
    First Reading: 1 John 2:29—3:6
    Gospel: John 1:29–34

The Gift We Really Want

On Christmas Day it's not uncommon for children to be asked, "Did Santa Claus bring everything you wanted?" The Christmas season has everything to do with gift giving because of the gift of love bestowed upon the world through the birth of Jesus. Our exchange of presents celebrates the presence that continues to remain with us so that we can "remain in him."

In today's First Reading St. John writes about the gift God has given us. It is an uncommon gift but is in fact the only thing our hearts have ever truly wanted: to be "God's children now." That which we have received from Christ both satisfies and purifies our hearts. We now can live as he lived and love as he loved, offering the same praise and thanksgiving Jesus offered to his Father, who has now become our Father as well.

In the Gospel St. John the Baptist greets Jesus as "the Lamb of God." The people who have come out to the Jordan for baptism hear in John's description a reference to sacrifice. For centuries the Israelites have been waiting for the lamb that God would provide in place of Isaac (see Genesis 22:8). John the Baptist is letting the people of Israel know that indeed their waiting has come to an end. God has visited his people.

John reveals Jesus as the one who has come to "take away the sin of the world." He knows that Jesus "is the one who will baptize with the Holy Spirit." The dove that hovers over Jesus fulfills what God told John before sending him on his mission:

"On whomever you see the Spirit come down and remain, he is the one who will baptize with the Holy Spirit."

This dove is a sign from God that the floodwaters of lawlessness and destruction (see Genesis 8:11) have become the waters of rebirth and regeneration. In this man whom John "did not know," God has chosen to recreate the world, so that all women and men can live the very righteousness of God.

Every year the Church gathers us together to celebrate, "with the harp and melodious song, with trumpets and the sound of the horn" (Responsorial Psalm, Psalm 98:5–6), the gift we have received in Christ Jesus the Lord. Love enabled him to take flesh of the Virgin Mary; love compelled John the Baptist to prepare the way for him; love is the key that unlocks our hearts to make room for him; and love alone is the saving power of God. Those who accept the gift of God's love can testify that Jesus is the Son of God and look forward in hope to that time when they shall "see him as he is."

The science of Love, ah, yes, this word resounds sweetly in the ear of my soul, and I desire only this science.

January 4
First Reading: 1 John 3:7–10
Gospel: John 1:35–42

What Are You Looking For?

The invitation extended to the two disciples of John the Baptist expresses perfectly the reason for which Jesus was born into the world—namely, that we would all finally be able to "see." Jesus isn't just inviting the two men to observe the place where he stays and the things he does there; he is offering them an entirely new way of knowing God, themselves, others, and all of creation. What they will "see" in spending time with Jesus will confirm that Jesus is in fact "the Lamb of God." It will move Andrew to search out his brother and say, "We have found the Messiah."

This is certainly a day the apostles will never forget. At "about four in the afternoon," the Son of God is revealed to them. No longer are they deceived about righteousness, because they experience for themselves that Jesus has come "to destroy the works of the Devil." The place to which this new "Rabbi" takes them is into the depths of their hearts, bringing such a radiant light that they leave everything and follow him (see Mark 1:17–18).

In the light of the Christmas season, we should ask ourselves if we have allowed Christ to take us to the place where he stays. Jesus came into the world so that we, too, might see. Jesus longs to open our hearts to the light of his life and the power of his love. This is the seed he has come to plant in our hearts. This is the seed of God that makes us his children.

In order for God's love to take root in our lives, we must leave everything that is not of God and follow Christ. This will protect us from being deceived by the "children of the Devil" and ensure that we remain "children of God."

At the beginning of Jesus's ministry, we learn the reason for his coming into the world. He has come to give us life! First he lets us see in our hearts whatever would stifle the power of God's love. Even if we sin, we know that we have an advocate in Christ (see 1 John 2:1). He has come not to destroy us but to save us.

The day Andrew left John the Baptist to follow after Christ, his eyes were opened to the truth about the anointed one for whom the people had been waiting. The Christmas season is a fitting time for us to once again open our eyes to the place where Jesus stays, the place where he has pitched his tent. That place is our hearts, and in the radiant light of this season, we should spend time with him there in joyful and prayerful conversation.

May all those who were not enlightened by the bright flame of faith one day see it shine.

January 5
First Reading: 1 John 3:11–21
Gospel: John 1:43–51

The Method of God

In the Gospel today we learn God's method for spreading the message that was heard "from the beginning." That method is "person by person."

"Jesus decided to go to Galilee," and there he finds Philip. (Philip most likely knows Andrew and Peter, because all three are from Bethsaida.) Jesus asks Philip to follow him. Philip in turn passes along this invitation to Nathanael, in words similar to those Christ used when he turned and saw Andrew following him: "Come and see."

The method for finding "the one about whom Moses wrote in the law, and also the prophets" has never changed. Those who "belong to the truth" have the responsibility to invite others to follow Christ. This act of love is a "righteous" work that confirms the love of God reigning in our hearts.

This love of God was revealed in that Jesus "laid down his life for us." God's method of spreading the Good News, person by person, will only succeed if we are willing "to lay down our lives for our brothers." As the apostle John reminds us in today's First Reading, we should love one another "not in word or speech but in deed and truth." This love lies at the heart of the "greater things" Jesus tells Philip he will see. It purifies our hearts so that they "do not condemn us."

Being a true child of God is the gift we receive during this holy season. Jesus comes to us again and again—through the sacraments, through his Word, in his teaching, and through the members of his body. He encourages us to keep following him.

Jesus sees us wherever we are, just as he saw Nathanael, and he wants for us only what in truth our hearts want: to see. No one wants to be, like Cain, a child of the evil one. We were created for the God who is greater than our hearts. We were created by love and for love.

In the words of Psalm 100, by the birth of Christ we have entered "his gates with thanksgiving" and "his courts with praise." We have been found by a love that will never disappoint or fail us, a love by which "we have passed from death to life." This love is not the result of pious sentiments, waxing and waning emotions, or profound spiritual and intellectual insights. It is a love that we experience in a personal way, in the way determined by God.

Andrew summoned Peter. Jesus summoned Philip, who summoned Nathanael. The celebration of Christmas offers us the chance to recall the person or people who have summoned us. It also strengthens us to go and do the same. By whatever means we possess, ours is the challenge to serve the Son of Man, who remains present in our brothers and sisters in need.

This is the mystery of my vocation, my whole life, and especially the mystery of the privileges Jesus showered upon my soul.

January 6

> (For use in countries where the Epiphany is celebrated on the
> Second Sunday After Christmas)
> First Reading: 1 John 5:5–13
> Gospel: Mark 1:7–11 or Luke 3:23–38

What Pleases God

A voice speaks from heaven in today's Gospel: The Father is pleased with his beloved Son.

The "water and Blood" flowing from the side of Christ have become the means by which God testifies on behalf of his Son. While Jesus willingly laid down his life as an act of love, his Father in heaven also willingly stepped back from intervening. The Father's act of love was to let his beloved Son die upon the cross. By way of it both the Father and the Son, in a sense, testify to each other.

God's singular desire is that we experience the abundant life meant for us from the beginning. That is why St. Luke's genealogy stretches all the way back to Adam. When God spoke the universe into existence, his Word had everything to do with our being baptized "with the Holy Spirit."

Unfortunately, sin disrupted God's plan. Now the baptism by which we share his life comes only through the humanity of the one "mightier" than John. The eternal life God longed to share with us in the beginning is now available through Jesus Christ. What God proclaimed to Jacob by way of ordinances and decrees, his Incarnate Son now articulates. In asking us to look backward, St. Luke is actually pointing us forward to where we, too, can stand with the "heavens being torn open" and hear the Father speak the same beautiful words to us: "You are my beloved."

The apostle John describes in his letter what most pleases the Father: our willingness to accept "the three that testify." Through the baptism inaugurated by Christ, each one of us has been born of water, blood, and the Holy Spirit. Each one of us has been incorporated into the life of the "victor over the world" and been given the eternal life that was meant to be ours from the beginning.

When "he was about thirty years of age," Jesus began his ministry of testifying to the truth. He did so by first descending into the waters of the Jordan in order to sanctify them for the Father's purposes. When the dove descended upon Jesus, John the Baptist knew that the splendor of God was unleashed in the world and that the peace for which his people had long prayed was present in the man whose sandal strap he was not fit to unfasten.

The ones who believe in the Son of God are those who dare to let the Father's voice thunder over them. Their hearts are aflame with the love to which the water and blood of Jesus testify. They willingly lay down their lives, just as Jesus and the Father laid down their lives, in mercy, generosity, and justice.

O Jesus, I know it, love is repaid by love alone.

January 7

(For use in countries where the Epiphany is celebrated on the
  Second Sunday After Christmas)
First Reading: 1 John 5:14–21
Gospel: John 2:1–11

What Should We Ask For?

Today the Mother of Jesus, attending a wedding at Cana in
Galilee, demonstrates her utter "confidence in God." This woman
who has fully given herself to God sees all things now with a
purity of heart that she truly expresses in a genuine love of
neighbor. This way of seeing results from the yes her life has
become, in every possible dimension. It is a fruit of the overshadowing of the Holy Spirit and the life of her Son, to whom she
has given her own flesh and blood.

Mary's purity of heart also lets her see in the plight of the
couple a reflection of the condition of humanity as a result of sin:
We lack the one thing that can cheer our hearts. Adam and Eve's
decision separated them from the life of God. This left us thirsting
for more than just water; it left us thirsting for divine life. The
wine so desperately needed to keep the wedding celebration
going is a symbol of that divine life for which we yearn.

This is why Mary brings the situation to her Son and why
Jesus's response is framed in terms of his "hour." Mary's entreaty
pierces her Son's heart: Jesus senses that she already anticipates the
moment when he will transform a cup of wine into the Blood of
the new and everlasting covenant. Mary can leave everything at
the feet of her Son. She knows that whatever he tells the stewards
to do will be "the beginning of his signs."

At a wedding at Cana in Galilee, Jesus reveals the extent to which "the Lord takes delight in his people" (Psalm 149:4). The Lord has "kept the good wine" of his divine life until now. Through the life, death, and resurrection of his Son, God will reveal how much he "loves his people." It is a revelation more surprising than that of the headwaiter as he tastes from the six stone jars.

At a wedding at Cana in Galilee, guests of the couple are literally able to taste the goodness of the Lord. This is because of the concern of the "Woman." Her love always unites the needs of others with the life of her Son.

Mary helps secure within our hearts the confidence that "if we ask anything according to [God's] will," it will be ours. She protects us from the evil one, and her constant prayer is that we remain in "the one who is true." Jesus her Son is the "true God and eternal life" of whom St. John writes.

Jesus's hour has come, and he shines light into every situation and circumstance of our lives. Jesus is the one who "adorns the lowly with victory" (Psalm 149:4). He fills our stone hearts with the wine of his divine life. In the blood of Christ, God reveals to us his glory.

Wasn't it before the wounds of Jesus, when seeing his divine blood flowing, that the thirst for souls had entered my heart?

Epiphany

Sunday Between January 2 and 8 (or January 6)

First Reading: Isaiah 60:1–6

Second Reading: Ephesians 3:2–3a, 5–6

Matthew 2:1–12

The Gift We Offer God

We can become so accustomed to hearing God's Word each Sunday that we fail to recognize "the newborn king of the Jews." We need a star to pierce the constellation of our lives with a radiant light, calling us to "rise up in splendor" and seek to pay him homage.

Most often this light that suddenly penetrates the dark drudgery of familiarity and obligation shines out of those who are "coheirs, members of the same body, and copartners in the promise in Christ Jesus." Like "magi from the east," they call us to the mystery celebrated today, that in Christ "we have been made new by the glory of his immortal nature" (Preface of Epiphany). Their willingness to prostrate their lives before the Lord and open the treasury of their hearts moves us to give to the child and his mother whatever they need from us.

At the star's appearance our hearts may be "troubled," but the sublime glory of the Lord is meant to shine over us. The birth of Christ is not a threat to our way of life but a sign of God's favor. In the town of Bethlehem, "by no means least among the rulers of Judah," the star stops over a place where there is no outward sign of majesty or power. The magi do not offer their gifts to a miracle worker, a mighty warrior, or a wise king. They present gold, frankincense, and myrrh to an innocent child—silent, at rest and at peace in his mother's arms. The humility of the scene proclaims the grandeur of God in a way no throne, no court, or no castle ever could.

Herod has nothing to fear from this "ruler who is to shepherd the people of Israel"; rather from him he has everything to gain. What will later be revealed by God's Spirit to the "holy apostles and prophets" of the new covenant is revealed to us in the quiet simplicity of these early days. The humility that marks the beginning of God's life as man will also mark its end.

Everything that takes place between the moment of Christ's birth and the horror of the cross will confirm what the magi witnessed when they found "the place where the child was." They returned to their country by another way, the Way that is also Truth and Life. All of us must "raise [our] eyes and look about." Today our light has come; the Lord has clothed us with his radiant beauty.

Ah! if this be so, Jesus, then enlighten me, for You know I am seeking only the truth.

Second Sunday After Christmas
(For use in countries where the Epiphany is celebrated on
January 6)
First Reading: Sirach 24:1–2, 8–12
Ephesians 1:3–6, 15–18
Gospel: John 1:1–18

Back to the Beginning

"In the beginning" the Creator of all things let loose his Spirit of
wisdom over the world. Everything God spoke into existence
through his Word is sustained in marvelous order and wondrous
beauty. All that came to be through the "Word [who] was with
God" points directly to the wisdom with which the universe was
created.

Yet in today's First Reading we learn that the "Spirit of
wisdom" was meant to dwell uniquely in Jacob's tent as God's
self-revelation. Israel's unique inheritance is being the people God
has chosen to share the truth of who he is. For Abraham's descendants wisdom is more than a knowledge of the created order. It
is an ever-widening grasp of the height and depth and breadth of
the God who made them "a glorious people."

In today's Second Reading St. Paul recalls for us the truth of
our humanity: "Before the foundation of the world," God chose
us for adoption as sons and daughters, through the same Word by
which all things came to be. This plan, formed long ago, is the
reason why God fixed a tent among his people. This free gift, this
"spiritual blessing in the heavens," is but the first movement of the
all-creating Word of God toward pitching his tent among
humanity. The "Word became flesh" so that God could speak for
himself, among the people he chose long ago, the truth that he is

love to the point of death. Only through the flesh and blood of the man Christ Jesus can the wisdom of God's love be revealed.

The celebration of Christmas is a celebration of the wisdom by which the heavens, the earth, and everything under the earth came to be. It is a celebration of the Creator's desire to be in loving communion with his creation through the life that is "the light of the human race." The celebration of Christmas is therefore a celebration of the cross, for it is in the death of the Son that the wisdom of God is definitively expressed. Through, with, and in Jesus we are able to live holy and blameless lives.

This, as St. Paul tells us, is in accordance with the Father's will. Through the Word, Incarnate of the Virgin Mary, we receive the spirit of wisdom. This gift grants us an ever-increasing knowledge of the one who has called us out of darkness and into his own wondrous light.

O my God, You surpassed all my expectations. I want only to sing of Your Mercies.

Monday After Epiphany (or January 7)
First Reading: 1 John 3: 22—4: 6
Gospel: Matthew 4: 12–17, 23–25

Everything Has Changed

Matthew's Gospel tells us that many of the people from "beyond the Jordan" followed Jesus as he went around Galilee. We recall from the Scriptures of Advent that this was where John preached repentance for the forgiveness of sin. Today we learn that John's arrest sends Jesus to "a land overshadowed by death" to fulfill the promise John made to those seeking his baptism. Jesus comes as a light, seeking those who are lost, with his own call to repentance and the proclamation that "the Kingdom of heaven is at hand."

For those following after Jesus, everything changes. Those who are sick with various diseases, lunatics, paralytics, the possessed, and all who are racked with pain are cured. The kingdom of heaven is a present reality and not an unearthly hope. People realize the epiphany of God's glory not in some spectacular sign but in the flesh and blood of the man Jesus. They believe in the name of God's Son, and Jesus assures them that they can indeed "keep his commandments."

The arrest of John signals the beginning of Jesus's ministry to announce that "we belong to God." Jesus is God come in the flesh, and as St. John tells us in today's First Reading, anyone who will not acknowledge this does not belong to God. It is through the humanity of Christ that God has chosen to define himself before the world.

We do not arrive at knowledge of God through our own thoughts and perceptions but through the Person by whom he has made himself known. And we only come to know Jesus by accepting the Spirit whom he has given us. It is the Spirit who educates us about the truth of God and of his Son, Christ Jesus. Through the Spirit united with our own, we have the capacity to do whatever pleases God. We remain in Christ by allowing him to continue sharing himself with us and showing us the truth of who we are.

Belonging to God changes everything. Certainly all those whom Jesus healed beyond the Jordan and throughout Galilee knew this. From the hand Jesus extends toward us, we have the chance to take hold of the light of life and let it shine within us. We can conquer the spirit of the antichrist, the demonic forces that attempt to make us question God and his unwavering love for us. By taking hold of the hand Jesus extends to us, we are united with the one who is greater than anything in the world, the one who has come to lead us to our eternal home.

Love never sees anything as impossible, for it believes everything is possible and everything is permitted.

Tuesday After Epiphany (or January 8)
First Reading: 1 John 4:7–10
Gospel: Mark 6:34–44

Jesus Satisfies Our Hunger

As we await the baptism of the Lord, the Scriptures foretell what we can expect from the one in whom the glory of God has been revealed. Today the Gospel intensifies the radiance of the light that has come into the world by reminding us about the purpose of Christ's coming: "His heart was moved with pity." Jesus came into this deserted world of ours knowing that we were hungry for God and that there was nothing we could purchase for ourselves that would satisfy that hunger. God sent his only begotten Son into the world to feed us with a food of which we did not know, the bread come down from heaven, his flesh for the life of the world.

The love expressed by Jesus in the Gospel is but a sign of the great love that will be his death upon the cross. Through his death Jesus will definitively prove to every nation on earth that "God is love." By the sign of the cross Jesus seeks to reassure us that God knows there is no end to our need for his love. That's why the twelve wicker baskets are filled with fragments: Jesus wants the crowds who have come and listened to his teaching to know that he will never allow them to go hungry.

The one who has been sent "as expiation for our sins" comes to us as a shepherd. He searches us out, and no matter how late it is when he finds us, he picks us up and brings us into the company of his fold (see Isaiah 40:11). As today's psalm tells us, Jesus leads us with "great care" and "governs [us] with justice." He "defends the afflicted" and "saves the children of the poor" (Psalm 72:2, 4).

God has sent his only begotten Son into the world in order to share with us the abundance of his everlasting life. All he asks is that we give ourselves to Jesus, no matter how meager, insufficient, or sinful we perceive ourselves to be. Jesus presents our lives to the Father. In a wonderful exchange of gifts—his life for ours and ours given to him—Jesus blesses us so that we are able to live more fully the love with which he first loved us.

The epiphany of God is the wondrous love of his only begotten Son. Jesus reveals himself in our nature so that we can more and more share his. By the power of his Spirit, he continues to gather us around himself, so that through word and sacrament we can eat and be satisfied. Through the Eucharist we share, God touches our lives and keeps his love alive within our hearts.

We are all worth more than five loaves and a few fish. If the Lord can feed a hungry multitude with them, then he can answer the world's hunger for love through us.

You desire to nourish me with Your divine substance and yet I am but a poor little thing who would return to nothingness if Your divine glance did not give me life from one moment to the next.

Wednesday After Epiphany (or January 9)
  First Reading: 1 John 4:11–18
  Gospel: Mark 6:45–52

Love Brought to Perfection

In today's First Reading the apostle John sums up well the message of Christmas: "Perfect love drives out fear." The vulnerable child wrapped in swaddling clothes and lying in a manger is an indisputable sign that God has not sent his only begotten Son as punishment. By looking upon the infant Jesus, we can know and believe in "the love God has for us."

While it's true that God has chosen to manifest his salvation in the most astounding way, human frailty and "hardened hearts" are no match for this child whom even the wind and sea will obey (see Matthew 8:27). God will not "pass by." The storms of life are calmed by the courage that comes from knowing that "God is love."

This is what the disciples in yesterday's Gospel failed to understand about the loaves and fishes. Jesus is in the world as the human face of the unseen God. He is the Father's kindness and compassion expressed through concrete acts of love of neighbor. Jesus did not come merely to teach us about God; he came to love us as God. The human family is God's neighbor!

The five thousand who "had eaten and were satisfied" represent every nation on earth. We have not been left alone to navigate the often tumultuous seas of life. Jesus is in the world! And we know that we remain in him if we are in the world in the same way.

No force of nature or cruel act of man can prevent the Lord from coming to us. The strength we draw from the innocent child instills within our hearts a peace that the world cannot give. From the moment Mary laid her Son in the manger, the Spirit of God was let loose in the world in a commanding way, the way of confidence and love. We are able to feed and clothe, comfort and care for the lowly and afflicted. The light that has come into the darkness of the "fourth watch" of human history casts out all fear. "Jesus is the Son of God," the "savior of the world."

Jesus made his disciples get into the boat in order to teach them that he would always be with them. Our lives are in the same boat, the Church. Christ is always with us. There is nothing to fear as we row toward the other side, to our eternal home.

Jesus is not a ghost but an abiding presence that is most apparent when we love one another. That's the only way we know that we "remain in him and he in us." "There is no fear in love"; there is only "confidence on the day of judgment."

He launched me full sail upon the waves of confidence and love.

Thursday After Epiphany (or January 10)
First Reading: 1 John 4:19—5:4
Gospel: Luke 4:14–22

Faith Is Victory

"Jesus returned to Galilee" and "came to Nazareth, where he had grown up." His goal was to educate people about the meaning of faith. As the incarnate presence of God's love, Jesus offers this education first to the people with whom he has spent his life.

So, "according to his custom," Jesus enters the synagogue and unfurls the truth that he is the Christ by reading a passage from the prophet Isaiah. What Jesus did that day in Nazareth, the Church has done for us throughout the season of Advent. Each day we heard a Scripture passage from Isaiah that taught us something about the child whose birth we were preparing to celebrate.

In the beautiful words of the prophet, we have a short but fitting description of what it means that Jesus is the Christ. We are told that the anointing by which he has become Messiah has the sole purpose of announcing "glad tidings." The Christ has come "to proclaim liberty to captives and recovery of sight to the blind, to let the oppressed go free."

These "gracious words" describe a God who cares for us and is attentive to our needs. The hope of eternal life has dawned on the world. The Father's only begotten Son has come to confront every form of human misery with a love that cannot be defeated.

"This Scripture passage" continues to be "fulfilled in [our] hearing" through our obedience to God's commandments. This the apostle John describes as loving our brother. There is no distinction between loving the God we "cannot see" and loving our brothers, because the Messiah is both God and our brother.

The one who claims to love God but hates his brother is therefore a liar.

By the "power of the Spirit," God's commandments are not burdensome. If we truly let God love us, then the education at Nazareth continues. We learn there that faith is not the same as belief. The people listening to Jesus in the synagogue believe in the Law, but they do not have faith in it. Jesus wants what they believe to become the foundation on which they will now build a life of faith.

Faith will determine our stance before the world. It will determine how we allow love to form and shape, lead, and guide every aspect of our lives. Let us believe that Jesus is the Christ and that we, too, have been begotten by God. This is the faith that "conquers the world."

I told myself that charity must not consist in feelings but in works.

Friday After Epiphany (or January 11)
   First Reading: 1 John 5:5–13
   Gospel: Luke 5:12–16

Made Clean

The simple gesture recorded in the passage from St. Luke is an epiphany of God. When Jesus stretches out his hand, the Father is reaching for the leper as well. Through Christ the Father is able to touch humanity with a compassion that heals the wretchedness and horror of our sinful condition. We no longer have to "wish" to be made clean, because the Father offers eternal life through the Person of his Son. All we have to do is allow Christ to touch us.

Sadly, fear often prevents us from prostrating ourselves before the Lord. What if Jesus cannot make me clean? What if I go on failing over and over again?

The Feast of the Epiphany demands that we no longer allow ourselves to be controlled by fear. "The one who came through water and Blood" gives us the assurance that we are not alone. Believing "in the name of the Son of God" makes it possible for us to look death and failure in the face and continue risking through love.

The Spirit who testifies to the truth generates in us the same selfless giving that epitomizes the life of Jesus. "The water and Blood" flowing from the Savior's side assure us beyond a doubt that God has risked everything on us. The cross definitively offers the Father's testimony to us. In the Person of his Son, God prostrates himself before us in a sense, calling us to be made whole by accepting his life.

In every town to which Jesus traveled, in every cure he worked, and in every word he spoke, the Father was present through, with, and in him. St. John tells us in the First Reading that acknowledging this is the foundation of faith, which makes us victors over the world. And Jesus teaches us in the Gospel that in order to strengthen our faith, we must have an intensive life of prayer. When we "withdraw…to pray," our lives conform more completely to the life of God's Son.

Through an interior life rooted in the Scriptures and grounded in Christ's teachings, our ability to speak with and listen to the Lord naturally deepens. This conversation, this ongoing pleading, is a fruit of the water and blood by which we have been given the Spirit and become members of Christ's body. It binds us to the community established in the Word made flesh and pushes us forward without fear, so that our lives become a perpetual testimony to the truth.

You see, dear Mother, that I am far from being on the way of fear.

Saturday After Epiphany (or January 12)
  First Reading: 1 John 5:14–21
  Gospel: John 3:22–30

Gift From Heaven

It seems clear from the Gospel that people understood the spiritual implications of baptism. Jesus and his disciples have no shortage of people coming to them in the region of Judea. This confuses the disciples of John. They already know that John is "not the Christ," but since John continues baptizing, they dispute the significance of the baptizing that Jesus is doing. Perhaps these baptisms are just "ceremonial washings."

The dispute presents John with an opportunity to make it clear that Jesus is the "bridegroom." The joy that made John leap in his mother's womb (see Luke 1:44) "has been made complete." He was sent to prepare the way before Christ, and this responsibility has been fulfilled. As the presence of Christ increases, John's life will indeed "decrease" to the point of imprisonment and death.

The gift from heaven is more than just cleansing from our sins. By referring to Jesus as "the one who has the bride," John anticipates St. Paul's explanation of the relationship of Christ with the Church (see Ephesians 5:32). John's characterization of Jesus also reinforces the words from today's First Reading, "We are in the one who is true, in his Son Jesus Christ."

John seems to understand that God wants to wed himself to us in Christ, such that we "belong to God." Through our shared nature with Christ, we can push from our lives the slightest traces of idolatry. Furthermore, we can ask for anything that is in accordance with the Father's will.

As we prepare to celebrate the baptism of the Lord, we are reminded that our baptism was more than a ceremonial washing. Although disputes about the importance of baptism continue, we should remain confident. Through water and the Holy Spirit, we have become new creations in Christ (see Romans 6:4). The false, idolatrous self that resulted from sin has not merely decreased; it has been put to death. Through the waters of baptism, the old order has passed away, and Christ has lavished upon us the grace of his divine life.

Human joy will only be complete in the wedding of the Bridegroom with his bride. In Christ we are united with God and with each other. God takes delight in his people individually and in the community begotten by his Son. As Psalm 149 today so beautifully points out, "This is the glory of all God's faithful."

A soul that is burning with love cannot remain inactive.

The Baptism of the Lord, Cycle A
First Reading: Isaiah 42:1–4, 6–7
Second Reading: Acts 10:34–38
Gospel: Matthew 3:13–17

The Gesture of Repentance
The season of Christmas concludes just as the season of Advent began: with words from the prophet Isaiah. The rich imagery of this great Old Testament figure prepared us to celebrate the coming of Christ as man and his return to us in glory. Today he describes for us the one who comes "from Galilee to John at the Jordan."

Jesus is God's "chosen one." He is literally the one upon whom God's spirit rests. Jesus is "a covenant of the people, a light for the nations." He does not shout or cry out, yet he comes "to establish justice on the earth." Long before the words "This is my beloved" sound from the heavens, they were written in the heart of the prophet and proclaimed by him.

Love leads Jesus to the Jordan to be baptized. The grace to "fulfill all righteousness" belongs to the sinless Son of God. The Baptist obediently acquiesces, confirming what St. Peter says to Cornelius in the Second Reading, "God shows no partiality."

By his willingness to be submerged in the waters of the Jordan, the whole of Jesus's life becomes a gesture of repentance. In humbling himself before John, Jesus humbles himself before the Father, and a new epiphany occurs. The heavens are opened, the Spirit descends upon the Son, and the Father voices his approval.

If the only begotten Son of the Father can lower himself for us and our salvation, then we should never be afraid to approach the Father in the same way. The Spirit of God has descended "like a dove" on all who are baptized into Christ Jesus. We have been drawn into the mystery of righteousness that has revealed itself as mercy. We should not fear doing good and even healing those oppressed by the devil.

The secret of the Little Way of spiritual childhood lies in the epiphany that occurred on Christmas morning in 1886. On that day thirteen-year-old Thérèse understood that God was speaking to her the words he spoke at Christ's baptism: "This is my beloved…, with whom I am well pleased."

I'm going to be doing only one thing: I shall begin to sing what I must sing eternally: "The Mercies of the Lord."

The Baptism of the Lord, Cycle B
First Reading: Isaiah 55:1–11
Second Reading: John 5:1–9
Gospel: Mark 1:7–11

The Opening of Heaven

Jesus comes "from Nazareth of Galilee," representing all those who are thirsty, poor, and hungry. The Father's only begotten Son has witnessed the conditions brought about by sin. He knows what it's like to spend money "for what is not bread" and "for what fails to satisfy." As he approaches the waters of the Jordan, he is prepared to show us once and for all that God "is generous in forgiving."

The journey to the Jordan began the moment Adam and Eve sinned. Their refusal to accept God's offer of friendship left the world infertile and void of that love that was meant to rain down from heaven. From the beginning the Father planned that his Word would go forth from his mouth to reconcile all things through our adoption into Christ. Through water and the Holy Spirit, we have become "children of God," the end for which God's Word was sent.

When we came "up out of the water" at our baptisms, the heavens opened for us as well. By the power of faith, our eyes have been opened to the truth the Baptist proclaims. If we remain united to the "one mightier than I" through obedience to his commandments, then the heavens will open ever more. We will then experience "the victory that conquers the world."

In Christ God comes to meet us and to satisfy our desire for the rich fare and choice food of his unfailing love. We should not be afraid to "seek the LORD" or to call upon him, because his

Word dwells among us through his body, the Church. Our adoption as daughters and sons of God signifies our acceptance into the great family that is the Christian community and ensures for us a way to the Father.

Through the waters of baptism, God has set a seal on our hearts. In him we can forsake the way of "the scoundrel" and banish all "wicked...thoughts." Through the waters of baptism, we become "confident and unafraid," as the Responsorial Psalm today tells us (Isaiah 12:2).

On the day of her profession, St. Thérèse of Lisieux composed a letter to Christ, asking that she never lose "the second robe of my baptism." Having heeded the words of the prophet Isaiah in today's First Reading, she wanted never to make even the slightest involuntary fault. She wanted to spend her life "conquering the world" through love. She hoped to be never a burden to the community but always a source of life through hidden sacrifices and countless little acts of love. Thus the waters of her baptism would pour out into the world, "giving seed to the one who sows and bread to the one who eats."

May Your will be done in me perfectly, and may I arrive at the place You have prepared for me.

The Baptism of the Lord, Cycle C
First Reading: Isaiah 40:1–5, 9–11
Second Reading: Titus 2:11–14; 3:4–7
Gospel: Luke 3:15–16, 21–22

In Solidarity With Sinners
In his first public act, Jesus makes it clear that he stands in solidarity with sinners. He goes to the place of "expectation" to be just another among the many being baptized by John. Already at the Jordan our Redeemer comes to us, subduing all things by his willingness to stand in line for "the bath of rebirth." The "one mightier than" John becomes powerless before him, in order to purify a people who will become God's very own.

The "glory" with which our Redeemer comes will be revealed through sacrifice. In the Jordan Jesus willingly lowers himself into the waters and is baptized with the Holy Spirit, who descends upon him in the form of a dove. Aflame with the Spirit, Jesus willingly lays down his life on the cross. He "gave himself for us" to show that the power "with which he comes" has everything to do with love. The Trinitarian moment recorded in the Gospel demonstrates that "the kindness and generous love of God" is the essence of the inner life.

The celebration of the baptism of Jesus is an opportunity for us to reflect on our own baptism. Paul's letter to Titus tells us that we have received the same Holy Spirit, the same fire! God's abundant life has been "richly poured out on us," like the cleansing waters that have made us God's own; indeed, they have made us his "heirs in hope of eternal life."

We should consider everything that happened between Jesus's baptism and the cross, in order that we might appreciate fully just how "the glory of the LORD shall be revealed." This will free us to give up everything that does not lead to God and banish all worldly ambitions.

The celebration of Jesus's baptism is the triumph of God's power revealed as "kindness and love." Christ's only ambition is to serve the Father's plan to reunite us to himself and preserve us from all wickedness. He does not burden us with anything he has not experienced. The Word speaks to the hearts of all people and has taken a place among them.

The life of St. Thérèse simply and clearly proclaims, "Here comes with power the Lord GOD." These glad tidings resonated from the heights of the mountains for her, because she accepted everything from the hand of God, including suffering.

Thérèse knew the epiphany of God that takes place in prayer. She was content throughout her short life to let Jesus shepherd her and was confident that he would lead her exactly where she needed to go. She looked forward to inheriting eternal life, because she already experienced heaven through her communion with God. She knew that he stood with her wherever she was.

...begging You to look upon me only in the Face of Jesus and in His heart burning with Love.

NOTES

Introduction

1. John Clarke, trans., *Story of a Soul: The Autobiography of St. Thérèse of Lisieux*, 3rd ed. (Washington, D.C.: ICS, 1996), p. 98.

2. See *Story of a Soul*, p. 17.

3. *Story of a Soul*, pp. 97–98.

Week One

Sunday, Cycle A: *Story of a Soul*, p. 277.

Sunday, Cycle B: *Story of a Soul*, p. 250.

Sunday, Cycle C: *Story of a Soul*, p. 157.

December 8, The Solemnity of the Immaculate Conception: *Story of a Soul*, p. 210.

Monday : *Story of a Soul*, p. 256.

Tuesday: *Story of a Soul*, p. 267.

Wednesday: *Story of a Soul*, p. 269.

Thursday: *Story of a Soul*, p. 219.

Friday: *Story of a Soul*, p. 245.

Saturday: *Story of a Soul*, p. 276.

Week Two

Sunday, Cycle A: *Story of a Soul*, p. 188.

Sunday, Cycle B: *Story of a Soul*, p. 234.

Sunday, Cycle C: *Story of a Soul*, p. 188.

December 12, The Feast of Our Lady of Guadalupe: *Story of a Soul*, p. 218.

Monday: *Story of a Soul*, p. 199.

Tuesday: *Story of a Soul*, p. 198.

Wednesday: *Story of a Soul*, p. 200.

Thursday: *Story of a Soul*, p. 214.

Friday: *Story of a Soul*, p. 219.

Saturday: *Story of a Soul*, p. 188.

Week Three

Sunday, Cycle A: *Story of a Soul*, p. 258.

Sunday, Cycle B: *Story of a Soul*, p. 79.

Sunday, Cycle C: *Story of a Soul*, p. 194 (both quotes in chapter).

Monday: *Story of a Soul*, p. 258.

Tuesday: *Story of a Soul*, p. 220.

Wednesday: *Story of a Soul*, p. 174.

Thursday: *Story of a Soul*, p. 174.

Friday: *Story of a Soul*, p. 197.

Week Four

Sunday, Cycle A: *Story of a Soul*, letter to Fr. Belliere, p. 267.

Sunday, Cycle B: *Story of a Soul*, p. 189.

Sunday, Cycle C: *Story of a Soul*, p. 214.

December 17: *Story of a Soul*, pp. 139–140.

December 18: *Story of a Soul*, p. 270.

December 19: *Story of a Soul*, p. 207.

December 20: *Story of a Soul*, p. 149.

December 21: *Story of a Soul*, p. 275.

December 22: *Story of a Soul*, p. 30.

December 23: *Story of a Soul*, p. 178.

Mass in the Morning on December 24: *Story of a Soul*, p. 136.

The Christmas Season: *Story of a Soul*, p. 98.

Vigil Mass for Christmas: *Story of a Soul*, p. 97.

Christmas Mass at Midnight: *Story of a Soul*, p. 99.

Christmas Mass at Dawn: *Story of a Soul*, p. 216.

Christmas Mass During the Day: *Story of a Soul*, p.188.

December 26, The Feast of St. Stephen: *Story of a Soul*, letter to Fr. Belliere, pp. 266–267.

December 27, The Feast of St. John the Evangelist: *Story of a Soul*, p. 155.

December 28, The Feast of the Holy Innocents, *Story of a Soul*, p. 213.

December 29, Fifth Day in the Octave of Christmas: *Story of a Soul*, p. 220.

December 30, Sixth Day in the Octave of Christmas: *Story of a Soul*, p. 97.

December 31, Seventh Day in the Octave of Christmas: *Story of a Soul*, p. 259.

Feast of the Holy Family, Cycle A: *Story of a Soul*, p. 128.

Feast of the Holy Family, Cycle B: *Story of a Soul*, p. 267.

Feast of the Holy Family, Cycle C: *Story of a Soul*, p. 129.

January 1, The Solemnity of Mary, Mother of God: *Story of a Soul*, pp. 40–41.

January 2: *Story of a Soul*, p. 195.

January 3: *Story of a Soul*, pp. 187–188.

January 4: *Story of a Soul*, p. 212.

January 5: *Story of a Soul*, p. 13.

January 6: *Story of a Soul*, p. 195.

January 7: *Story of a Soul*, p. 100.

Epiphany: *Story of a Soul*, p. 197.

Second Sunday After Christmas: *Story of a Soul*, p. 208.

Monday After Epiphany (or January 7): *Story of a Soul*, pp. 160–161, quoting Thomas à Kempis, *The Imitation of Christ*, bk. 3, chap. 5.

Tuesday After Epiphany (or January 8): *Story of a Soul*, p. 199.

Wednesday After Epiphany (or January 9): *Story of a Soul*, p. 174.

Thursday After Epiphany (or January 10): *Story of a Soul*, p. 222.

Friday After Epiphany (or January 11): *Story of a Soul*, p. 173.

Saturday After Epiphany (or January 12): *Story of a Soul*, pp. 257–258.

The Baptism of the Lord, Cycle A: *Story of a Soul*, p. 13.

The Baptism of the Lord, Cycle B: *Story of a Soul*, p. 275 (both quotes in chapter).

The Baptism of the Lord, Cycle C: *Story of a Soul*, p. 276.

ABOUT THE AUTHOR

Fr. Gary Caster, a priest of the Diocese of Peoria, Illinois, is the Catholic chaplain at Williams College in Massachusetts. He leads retreats and parish missions, has written and produced shows for EWTN, and has contributed articles to various publications, including *Magnificat*. He is the author of *Mary: In Her Own Words* and *The Little Way of Lent: Meditations in the Spirit of St. Thérèse of Lisieux*.